THE POWER OF LOVE

THE
POWER
OF LOVE

Overcoming the Love
of Power in Your
Relationships

DAVID CONGO, Psy.D.,
and JANET CONGO, M.A.

MOODY PRESS
CHICAGO

All Scripture quotations, unless indicated, are taken from the *Holy Bible: New International Version*®. NIV®. Copyright © 1973, 1978, 1984 International Bible Society. Used by permission of Zondervan Publishing House. All rights reserved.

Verses marked (TLB) are taken from *The Living Bible* © 1971. Used by permission of Tyndale House Publishers, Inc., Wheaton, IL 60189. All rights reserved.

Verses marked (RSV) are taken from the *Revised Standard Version of the Bible* © 1962, 1973 by Oxford University Press, Inc. and are used by permission. All rights reserved.

Verses marked (NKJV) are taken from *The New King James Version*. Copyright © 1979, 1980, 1982, Thomas Nelson, Inc., Publishers.

Verses marked (KJV) are taken from the King James Version.

The use of selected references from various versions of the Bible in this publication does not necessarily imply publisher endorsement of the versions in their entirety.

ISBN: 0-8024-6324-X

1 3 5 7 9 10 8 6 4 2

Printed in the United States of America

To our son Christopher and daughter Amy.

You have taught us so much about loving and relating.
You have helped us face areas in our lives
in which we needed to grow.
You have brought delight to our hearts.
You have added warmth to our home.

CONTENTS

FOREWORD

Power and Love

Power and love are wonderful and horrible. They are exhilarating and frightening. They can be awesomely used or abused.

Insecure men and women in today's society find themselves in a never-ending, rat-race pursuit of power, illicit sex, and money—and the primary motive for the illicit sex and money is ultimately even more power.

And yet it is our God-given responsibility to develop fully our loving spirit of power and our powerful spirit of love. We are emotional and spiritual beings, made in God's image. Power and love are vital components of who we are becoming.

Dave and Jan Congo are not only close personal friends, but also excellent insight-oriented therapists who quickly cut through the superficial surface issues to get to the genuine core issues of concern in our human relationships.

Whether it be in marriage, in the workplace, in our church relationships, or in our neighborhoods, Dave and Jan Congo have developed valuable tools that we can all use to transform our own areas of loveless power and powerless love into powerful love. They also teach us defensive skills to protect ourselves from being abused by the overly controlling, loveless power of others. I highly recommend this book to assist each of us in the never-ending journey of becoming the powerful and loving persons God wants us to become.

PAUL MEIER, M.D.
Co-founder of the
Minirth-Meir Clinics

ACKNOWLEDGMENTS

A Word of Thanks

We learn about loving not by studying, but by listening to and being accepted by powerful lovers. Several of them appear in this volume, most behind names not their own. We thank them for sharing their lives with us. Some we need to highlight.

Lela Gilbert, a gifted writer and encourager, who lifted two grieving people with her friendship, her writing skills, her creativity, and her belief in this project.

Dr. Paul and Jan Meier, treasured friends, who demonstrate powerful love individually and personally. A special thanks to Dr. Meier for writing the foreword.

Dr. H. Norman Wright, a mentor and powerful forgiver in our personal journey.

Dr. and Mrs. Eugene Coffin, who through their marriage of fifty-six years have taught us much by example.

Our parents, Dr. and Mrs. Howard Shanta and Mr. and Mrs. Herb Congo, for their loving support.

The Lord Jesus Christ, the ultimate example of *powerful love.*

1

TAKING A POWER TRIP

Greta was out of town on business—again. A single mom as well as a successful executive, she was usually able to be at home with her school-age children. However, another trip to Vancouver, British Columbia, had forced her to leave her son and daughter behind with Grandma. She always felt vaguely guilty when she was away, and Greta was relieved that this ten-day trip was nearly over. Three more days and she would be back to stay. She smiled as she picked up the phone and dialed home.

"Hi, Mom . . ." There was a hint of unhappiness in her twelve-year-old son's voice.

"What's wrong, Jeremy?"

There was a brief pause. "Oh, it's just Ms. Hennessy . . ."

Jeremy was, if anything, overly conscientious about his school work. He was a straight A student, and Greta had few worries about his school performance. "What about Ms. Hennessy?" Greta recognized the name of his social studies teacher.

"Well, she gave us a special project assignment today— it's due Friday. I'm supposed to make an ancient Egyptian musical instrument. That only gives me three days, and I have to go to a craft store to buy the stuff to make it. Grandma doesn't even know where a craft store is, so I can't do it till you get back. But Ms. Hennessy says we get F's if we don't turn it in Friday. That means my grade will drop to a B + ."

Greta groaned inwardly. *How do they come up with these ideas, anyway? Two years ago it was a California mission. Last year it was a medieval costume. Now they want an ancient Egyptian musical instrument?*

She sighed. "Don't worry about it, Jeremy. I'll fax her a note saying you'll do it when I get back. I'm sure she'll understand."

"Mom, Ms. Hennessy hates notes from parents. You know that!"

Greta faintly remembered having sent a note earlier in the year complaining about the volume of homework Jeremy was bringing home—sometimes more than two hours a night. Ms. Hennessy had scowled fiercely as she read the note, then had snapped, loud enough so the whole class could hear, "You can tell your parents to stop sending me notes about homework. I'll decide for myself how much homework you should be doing!"

"Well, Jeremy, I don't know what else I can do besides sending a note."

"But what if I get an F anyway?"

"I don't think that's going to happen."

After saying good-bye to Jeremy, Greta wrote out a note on her letterhead.

Dear Ms. Hennessy,
    Would you please extend Jeremy's special project deadline until I return from British Columbia? I am out of town on business and won't be back until Friday night. He has no way to get to the craft store, and no money to purchase the materials for the musical instrument. His grade is very important to him, and I would appreciate your consideration.
    Thank you for extending his deadline until Monday.
    Sincerely,
    Greta Jameson

Greta faxed the note to the school the following morning. When she called home that night, Jeremy sounded more downcast than ever. He said, "Mom, Ms. Hennessy read the fax to the class. Then she said, 'Jeremy, I don't like the way your mother wrote this note to me. She started out with a request and ended with a statement. I don't like parents telling me how to run my classroom!'"

A quiet, shy boy, Jeremy had been deeply humiliated. And Greta was enraged. "I'll call her when I get back, Jeremy," she said, trying to hide the anger in her voice. "But did she extend the deadline till Monday?"

"Yeah. She said, 'I don't mind giving you extra time, but next time tell your mom to ask me not tell me.'"

Greta dialed the school office first thing Monday morning. When Ms. Hennessy called her back, Greta said, "I wanted to discuss my fax with you. Jeremy tells me you were unhappy with the way it was worded."

"Yes. I didn't appreciate your telling me what to do."

Greta's hands were trembling. Bitter, insulting words were racing through her mind, and she was trying desperately not to say them out loud. "Well I didn't appreciate your embarrassing my son in front of the classroom, either. Next time you have something to say to me, please speak to me directly. Don't involve Jeremy."

Ms. Hennessy's response was icy. "I'll run my classroom anyway I want! I don't need advice from you about homework or about what I say to my students. I would have given Jeremy more time anyway because I'm a reasonable person. But I'm the teacher, not you. It's my classroom, and these are my students. Don't tell me what to do!"

Although Greta succeeded in getting Jeremy's project postponed, she was infuriated by the unpleasant encounter with Ms. Hennessy. Even though she reported it to the principal, a troublesome feeling lingered throughout the weekend. Somehow her boundaries had been crossed. Her rights had been violated. Ms. Hennessy had seized authority over her, rebuked her, and hurt her son in the process.

We are surrounded by people who feel a need to be in control. We may find them in the classroom, in our marriages, in the workplace, in the church, among friends, or among siblings. Sometimes, we may even see a controller gazing back at us from the bathroom mirror. Controllers want to control people and circumstances and will use power games in innumerable ways to achieve their ends. The power they seek is thus a destructive power. Put another way, we can say:

*Destructive power is power dedicated
to controlling people and circumstances.*

Destructive power is power without love. It is manipulative and coercive, and as such, it creates untold agony. Its goal is the continuation of the controller's role, and it strongly resists repentance or reform. "I don't want to change—you change!" Destructive power obstructs both personal transformation and reconciliation.

As we can see from Greta's story, controllers can leave in their wake hurt feelings and troubled minds. Sad to say, their behavior can also result in broken hearts and, not infrequently, bruised and battered bodies. The impact on their victims is evident. But what happens to the person who uses destructive power?

HOW DESTRUCTIVE POWER CORRUPTS

First of all, destructive power corrupts the person using it. A controller becomes a law unto himself (or herself—there are no gender limitations to being a controller; it is an equal opportunity role). Controllers convince themselves that they are "right" and anyone with a different opinion is "wrong." Their world is black and white. And they are accountable to no one.

Even objective truth is not allowed to stand in the way of the controller's behavior. Truth is either misrepresented through innuendo and exaggeration, or it is thoroughly denied to support the controller's stance. In another classroom episode, we find a student being the controller.

Bill was a young man who came into therapy trying to overcome his own use of destructive power. He described one particular occasion during his college days when he had failed to complete a paper on time. Instead of facing the consequences of his inefficiency, he arrived in class that day with an empty manila folder. When he entered the room, he made himself conspicuous by intentionally creating a commotion, making sure everyone knew he was there.

When his professor collected the assignments, Bill turned in his empty folder, which he carefully placed in the middle of the pile. Days later, the professor returned the graded assignments to the class—Bill's was marked with a large, red F.

Bill threw a fit. He asked the other students, "You saw me turn in my paper, right? Don't you remember? That was the day I . . ." and he reminded them of the commotion he'd caused coming into class. He proceeded to humiliate the professor, accusing him of losing the paper, even questioning his competency in front of all the other students.

The professor, who by now was beginning to feel insecure about his own version of the story, quieted Bill by agreeing to average his other grades, to ignore the F, and to do whatever was necessary to resolve the "misunderstanding." The paper never got written, and truth did not triumph. On the other hand, Bill, the controller, was successful in his selfish attempt to influence another's behavior to his advantage.

Besides, Bill got a good laugh from his friends every time he told the story.

LONELY AT THE TOP

Being a controller is a lonely business. Controllers distance and isolate themselves from others. This happens because destructive power creates a form of one-upmanship. It is interested in self-advancement at any cost, and is often fueled by unapologetic selfishness. We found this particular aspect of control in the workplace vividly illustrated in Michael Korda's books *Power! How to Get It, How to Use it* and *Success! How Every Man and Woman Can Achieve It.*[1]

Korda is an English-born, Oxford-educated book editor based in New York and a spokesperson for women's rights. His writings depict sophisticated corporate society with its impeccable clothes, "I-win-you-lose" tactics, and chic, contemporary status symbols. Korda claims that striving for success is "the ultimate turn-on."

How does the well-heeled world of the successful man or woman operate? In Korda's view, it is an environment full of insecurity in which we need to adopt a defensive posture because everyone else is trying to do us in. Manipulation is alive and well, and our goal is to keep everyone off balance. Our greatest competitors (which amount to enemies) are people who question us, whether they be co-workers, colleagues, or spouses. The ultimate fool, according to Korda, is the person who works hard without trying to impress others.

And, in case you ever wondered whether it really is "lonely at the top," in Korda's own words, the true test of success is the "degree to which one can isolate from others."

CONTROL: VISIBLE AND INVISIBLE

Besides isolating themselves, controllers try to keep their reality predictable and will do anything it takes—overtly or covertly—to keep things the same.

Sometimes in full sight and earshot of others, parents or partners scream, curse, criticize, threaten, employ sarcasm, make cutting remarks, mock, intimidate, ignore, use physical force, or practice sexual exploitation. Ironically, we've learned that often the more coercive the manipulation, the more dependent is the one using it.

Consider, for example, the husband who doesn't get what he wants sexually from his wife. She walks into the bedroom, and finds him holding a gun to his head, threatening to kill himself. "I've got to have you! I'd rather be dead." His hope: the wife will be intimidated into intimacy—a desperate measure to be sure, and an obvious one.

Not so obviously, even invisibly, some individuals bring into play something we therapists call passive-aggressive behavior. This is best illustrated by the humorous picture of a massive, wagging Saint Bernard puppy who puts his paws on your shoulders, licks your face, and goes to the bathroom on your shoe—all at the same time. Overeager, poorly trained puppies can be excused for their behavior. Passive-aggressive people are less innocent. They disguise their control and hostility in an assortment of clever ways.

Slender and dark-eyed, Maria described her first date with her ex-fiancé, Carlos, when she weighed a little more but was still slim. One moonlit night he said softly, "You know Maria, I don't usually fall for women who look heavy like you." From that moment on, and for the duration of their three-year relationship, Maria suffered continuous blows to her self-esteem.

Sometimes her lover would poke her (affectionately, of course) in the stomach and simply roll his eyes. Or he would raise his eyebrows when she'd stir sugar in her coffee or order desserts. Never once did Carlos compliment her, no matter how much she tried to look her best.

"I must be fatter than I think I am," she'd think to herself, studying her very attractive reflection in the mirror.

As months passed, Maria grew increasingly self-conscious, and lost fifteen pounds she really didn't need to lose. Predictably, the relationship wasn't improved by the weight change. Finally she broke up with Carlos, and promptly regained the fifteen pounds. When he next saw her, using a reverse tactic, he studied her with a concerned expression on his face. "Have you been sick?" he inquired. "You're so thin . . . maybe you need to put on a few pounds."

Passive-aggressive people are also beautifully illustrated in the Scripture passage about the two sons who were given work instructions by their father (Matthew 21:28–31). The first one said, "No, I won't go!" but had second thoughts and obeyed. The second one smiled and said, "Sure! No problem Dad." But he never showed up for work. His behavior was clearly passive-aggressive.

"Which one," Jesus asked, "was the most obedient?"

Here are some typical passive-aggressive statements.

- "Angry? Me? I'm not angry."
- "Nothing . . . I'm just thinking."
- "I'm just being honest."
- "I don't hate it."
- "What's the problem?"
- "I won't stop you."
- "Can't you take a joke?"
- "You take things too personally."

A passive-aggressive spouse doesn't want children so she refuses to have sex.

A passive-aggressive executive calls an emergency meeting and then shows up thirty minutes late.

A passive-aggressive husband accompanies his successful wife to a corporate dinner. She is chatting happily with her business partners when he walks up beside her and says in a stage whisper, "Shhh . . . you're talking too much," just loud enough for everyone to hear. He succeeds in making her feel ridiculous. Meanwhile he looks knowledgeable at her expense.

Passive-aggressives find it difficult to

- Say "No."
- Get angry.
- Meet deadlines.
- Say "I need you."

TRYING TO PLAY GOD

Whether passive-aggressive or overtly demanding, controllers have no concept of how far they push other people, carelessly trampling other's personal boundaries underfoot. They don't have any sense of where they stop and the other person begins. Instead, they believe that they have the right to re-create others into their own "Revised Standard Version." They have no tolerance for individual rights or differences.

We've already noted that controllers isolate themselves. But they also find themselves further isolated because they destroy valuable relationships. Their actions and attitudes remove integrity, trust, and dialogue from the script. They are always right, always central to the story, always superior in attitude; why bother to have a conversation?

In a religious environment or a Christian setting the controller becomes his own deity, stretching his desire to manipulate even into the heavens. He (or she) tells God what He needs to do, when He needs to do it, and in what manner it must be done.

When God shows Himself to be anything but a puppet on a string, the controller is filled with rage toward Him. He may even turn his back on his religion when his own personal omnipotence comes into question. Sometimes this is acted out in "name-it-and-claim-it" churches and Bible studies. There faith is placed in one's own faith, not in a personal, caring God who alone has the right to be in control of everything and everybody.

Being a controller is a thankless job. And playing God is a hopeless endeavor. So why do we do it? (And let's face it, all of us join the ranks of controllers from time to time.) Why do we stay in the controller position when we know we really can't control anyone or anything?

WHY WE STAY IN CONTROL

EXPECTATION OF REWARDS

For one thing, being in the controller position works—at least temporarily. Controllers get what they want when they want it. This provides immediate gratification.

Controlling often provides a temporary boost to our sagging self-esteem. In relationships, the underfunctioning of one person allows the other person to overfunction. This sort of hyperactive busyness has an ego-bolstering effect on the controller. The helpless and dependent stance taken by the one-down person causes the other person to develop what Murray Bowen calls a "pseudo-self."[2]

This was acted out in the life of Jessica. She had a long and abusive marital history with Brett, which included violent beatings and occasional murder threats. She finally separated from him because she feared for her life and the lives of her children. Brett's response was to have her utilities disconnected, to refuse any financial support, and to harass her day and night.

Jessica lost her job because of Brett's insane behavior— he had called her boss and glibly convinced him that she was embezzling company funds.

Finally, penniless and with no family to help her, Jessica agreed to be reunited with her abusive husband. Resigned to hopelessness, she simply assented to submit totally to him, a posture their pastor wholeheartedly endorsed. "Everything will be fine if you'll just let him be the head of the house," he smiled.

Brett was delighted, quite convinced that Jessica had come back because she loved him and had seen the error of her ways. In fact, nothing could have been farther from the truth, as time was soon to tell. In the meantime, however, Brett enjoyed immediate gratification as the primary result of his controlling actions.

"CONTROL OR BE CONTROLLED" SYNDROME

There are other reasons that we remain in control. We may have learned our behavior in a childhood home where Mom or Dad provided a controlling role model. Perhaps we're still trying to earn a parent's approval. We might also have learned our habits within a peer group, because of a mentor or a boss at work, or for some other reason.

Controlling sometimes continues because we reason, consciously or unconsciously, "Unless I control, I will be controlled." Perhaps we grew up in the home of an arrogant dictator or were in a past relationship in which we experienced no personal power. Now we promise ourselves, *Never again!* No more will we revert to that dependent, helpless victim stance. This is a pendulum-swing reaction.

FEAR OF VULNERABILITY

A controller may also be afraid of his own vulnerability. He views any personal need as a sign of weakness, and he must not be weak. Either that is how he felt growing up or that is how he viewed an abused parent. Painful as it is to watch one parent being abused by another, a child often develops a contempt for the parent who couldn't defend or take care of herself or himself.

A capable young businesswoman said to her fiancé, "When I feel like I need you, I feel like you're going to control me and I'll lose myself. I don't want to need you! It makes me feel weak, and when I feel weak then I think you're going to reject me, the way my mom rejected my dad."

Because controllers are afraid of being needy or weak, they stifle the neediness in themselves. They remain aware only of their aggressive, strong characteristics. What a setup this is for attracting "weak" partners! In relationships with dependent partners, controllers vicariously get in touch with their own neediness. After awhile, however, controllers revert back to hating the needy part of themselves. Before long, that hate is directed towards the dependent person.

FEAR OF ABANDONMENT

Controllers are often terrified of being abandoned. This conflict between love and fear probably dates back to early childhood. Perhaps as early as infancy, the person learned "Love means I will be hurt, engulfed, abandoned, deprived, or abused." How frightening a love relationship seems to this person!

Unconsciously the decision is made, perhaps by a husband, to make a wife less powerful. "If I can damage her self-esteem, she will be dependent on me, and will become too weak to leave me. Then I won't have to be so afraid of being abandoned."

Fathers tell their attractive daughters they cannot wear make-up, or refuse to allow them to date. Pastors warn of eternal consequences if other doctrines are explored, hoping to keep their flocks intact. Bosses play this game too, by tearing down the confidence of their employees. In doing so, they attempt to keep them from seeking better opportunities.

"I DESERVE THE BEST" SYNDROME

Some controllers cherish a sense of entitlement. They honestly believe that they deserve to have everything work out their way. When things don't perfectly suit them, they become angry. They sabotage whatever remains, calling it "bad."

This individual feels that he (or she) deserves to have every need catered to. He expects to be comforted, nurtured, soothed, admired, encouraged, listened to, sympathized with, and supported. This controller may have been an only child whose parents met every need before it was even voiced. When controllers assume this position of privilege, they are ungrateful for anything that is done for them. After all—why shouldn't they have what they want?

This sense of entitlement may expand to the point that the controller begins to feel omnipotent. *I'm like God,* he tells himself. *I deserve the best and I know what everyone else needs, too.* Whether this attitude stems from pride or injury, it is dangerous—not only to the controller, but to the ones he tries to control. One who seeks to usurp God's power and authority can only fail.

One look at Jackie, and even an untrained eye could see fear flickering across her face, the lack of self-confidence, the victim's pain. When Jackie came for counseling, her emotions were deeply scarred. Some years before, she had been placed in a foster home because of mistreatment she had suffered at the hands of her parents. Her life was in continuous disarray, and she couldn't seem to find her place in the world.

Although the legal system had rescued her from further tragedy in her family home, that rescue didn't happen soon enough to prevent the wounds that had already occurred. She was the eldest of four in a family that believed in good education—to a fault. In her parents' opinion, the state school system was ill-equipped to make the most of their children's intellectual gifts. So they home-schooled their sons and daughters.

If Jackie watched television, she was required to write a report on the show she watched. Her instruction continued through every waking hour. But she was responsible not only for her own scholastic pursuits, but many other tasks as well. Because she was thought to be the brightest, she was expected to supervise her brothers and sisters and, just in case she ran out of things to do, she served as housekeeper too.

Of course it was impossible for her to accomplish everything well—there weren't enough hours in the day and she didn't have enough energy. But when she failed to meet her parents' outrageous standards, she paid a high price. She was grabbed by the hair and jerked around painfully. If she cried out, her mother shoved her to the floor and covered her mouth with her hand so firmly that the terrified girl couldn't get a breath of air.

When Jackie's father arrived home from work, the story of her failure, whatever it was, was recounted to him, and he began the punishment process all over again by ripping off his belt, backing Jackie into a corner and beating her. Sometimes he handed the belt to the younger children, and ordered them to beat her too.

On one occasion, her mother ripped to shreds all the clothes in Jackie's closet and drawers and then lied to her husband about it, saying that the girl had angrily destroyed her own wardrobe. Her brothers and sisters were given scissors and told to cut Jackie's hair because she had displeased her parents. She was locked out of the house and left in the backyard for hours on end. This sort of activity persisted until concerned neighbors finally called for help and the Child Protective Services got involved.

Years later, Jackie was still seeking help in therapy.

Clearly hers is an extreme example, but even her terrible child abuse was motivated by something—a rationale that caused Jackie's parents to continue their evil behavior. Whether it was a sense of entitlement, a need to play God, or a twisted pride in their children's accomplishments, the damage they did to Jackie will be with her for the rest of her life.

Frequently, controllers are blind to others' needs. They suffer tunnel vision to such a degree that they are unaware of the effect their controlling has upon others. They hear and see only what they want. Such individuals are captive to their own rigid biases and are always opinionated and defensive.

INTERNALIZED RAGE AND LACK OF CONTROL

Internalized rage may cause controlling, which is used as a self-protective device. A child who is raised by an authoritarian tyrant is never allowed to separate from the parent in any way. To be different or separate is viewed by the rigid, narrow overbearing parent as betrayal. The child isn't allowed to make mistakes, to form his or her own attitudes and opinions, or to express any anger—only the dictator has that right. Therefore the child's anger goes underground and is stored internally. It is as if it goes into hibernation, only to be awakened in some other relationship when it emerges as control. It serves to insulate the person against exposure and it keeps others away.

In other cases, aspects of the controllers' lives may be so out of control that they assume undue authority in other relationships. Perhaps the marital relationship is destructive and shaming. The frustrated spouse therefore becomes a tyrant in the workplace, in the church, or in a parenting role.

IGNORANCE AND SELFISHNESS

If the dictator happens to be a Christian man, he may choose to stay in the controller position because of a combination of selfishness, ignorance, and false ideas of male headship. (We'll discuss this further in chapter 3.) His wife's or female employee's job is to make him feel good, pump up his ego, and adore him.

Prejudice pollutes his thinking. He excuses his behavior by citing 1 Peter 3, in which women are called the "weaker partners" ("weaker vessels" in the KJV). He uses this passage, and other similar out-of-context Bible verses, to prove that he is superior to women. He may belittle his female co-workers, and fondly refer to his wife as the "little woman."

Marge meekly raised her hand at a Christian seminar to ask a pertinent question. "What do you do," she inquired hesitantly, "when you and your husband disagree about child rearing? Or about disciplining the children?"

The leader was about to answer when Marge's husband spoke out in a rather booming voice, "Well, my dear, that is a submission issue," he announced, causing laughter to ripple across the room at Marge's expense.

Of course the poor woman felt humiliated—that was her husband's intention. The truth is, Marge was not dealing with a submission issue, but a control issue. She and her husband were involved in a power struggle with each other. And the outcome is inevitable: they will do incredible damage to their children if they don't stop.

Often a woman doesn't recognize a man's underlying feelings of low self-esteem. She falls in love with what appears to be a "strong" man's confidence. Psychologist Rudolf Dreikurs discovered that behaviors chosen by partners with low feelings of self-esteem are generally directed towards these activities: excusing themselves for shortcomings, attracting attention, gaining power, and enacting vengeance.

Because of incomplete and unfortunate teaching, many Christian women also believe the Bible teaches that husbands are supposed to control their wives, and that wives in turn are supposed to obey their husbands in all things. This teaching blinds women to the reality that overcontrol is a statement of the husband's personal inadequacies, not his rightful role.

Chuck sat in Dave's presence one day and informed him that if his wife would just submit, everything would be fine. To make his point, he slammed his King James Bible down on Dave's desk. Chuck and his wife had separated because of his constant physical abuse and his involvement with another woman. Now he felt it was "of the Lord" for them to be reconciled.

With that in mind, Chuck had invited his wife over the evening before the session. After a lovely candlelight dinner he presented his plan of reconciliation. She was lukewarm to the idea, and an argument followed. Their words become more and more heated. She fled from the house, only to have Chuck follow her and push her to the ground with such force that her neck was bruised. She finally escaped after a violent struggle.

There was no remorse in Chuck's voice or body language. He simply believed that if she would submit, their problems would cease.

Ann Landers once printed a letter from Big Ed, who stated that some women are like dumb animals. You have to show them who's boss. He said he was training his own wife, "and believe me, there are no arguments in our house. This is the way all families ought to be run." (And all those controlling husbands we call "married bachelors" said "Amen.")

Any spiritualized put-down of women is thoroughly unbiblical. But we see it in churches throughout the world. In his thought-provoking book *The Mystery of Marriage*, Mike Mason write these words: "'A man's home is his castle,' goes the saying, and in practice this is taken to mean that a man is allowed and even encouraged to develop into any sort of despot or devil he likes within the cozy confines, the cordoned lawlessness, of his own family. After all, aren't his loved ones those who 'understand' and 'accept' him? And so marriage becomes a form of institutionalized complacency, a hothouse of mutually nourished neuroses. Love is even construed to be a sort of carte blanche approval for all kinds of selfishness and evil, a dispensation giving two people special license to sin against one another."[3]

This acting out of false theology represents not a loving interaction but a monologue. This kind of man doesn't take a wife, he takes a hostage.

WHAT ABOUT YOU? WHAT ABOUT ME?

All this leads us to one big question: Am I a controller? How controlling *are* you? Think about these statements and see if any of them apply.

1. I get upset when I don't get my own way.
2. I am exasperated by others' lack of insight.
3. I expect to make the final decision on every issue related to our home.
4. I am adept at influencing other people's opinion.
5. I have an unusual capacity to make right decisions.
6. I am exceptionally perceptive at judging people's character.
7. When things are out of control, I feel uniquely qualified to manage the situation.
8. I have little patience with other people's incompetence.
9. I feel angry when my idea is voted down.
10. I crave competition.
11. I often feel like others don't do their part.
12. I am a leader.
13. I am convinced that my beliefs are always right.
14. I find listening to other people's perspectives annoying.
15. I know what is best for others.
16. Rather than forcing my views on others, I become silent and withdrawn.

17. I use Scripture references to attack others or their position.

18. I am compelled to have the last word.

19. I value logic more than emotion.

20. I never let my guard down.

21. I have a difficult time asking for help.

22. I always hold the TV remote control.

23. I find it difficult to take no for an answer.

24. Winning is very important to me.

25. I react defensively when others question my choices or opinions.

You may find that many of these statements apply to you. Or you may be shouting, "Boy, is that ever my husband to a T!" Or you may be thinking of your child, parent, officemat,e or friend. Chances are, however, the picture is a bit more complex than it may first appear to be. Curiously, even if we are extremely controlling, we are also very dependent. We are complicated and contradictory creatures, rarely a "pure" example of either control or compliance.

There are two sides to every story. And there's more to dependency and adult victimization than meets the eye. To begin to understand the people who allow themselves to be controlled, take a look at chapter 2.

NOTES

1. Michael Korda, *Power! How to Get It, How to Use it* (New York: Ballantine, 1987); *Success! How Every Man and Woman Can Achieve It* (New York: Random, 1987).

2 Murray Bowen, *Family Therapy in Clinical Practice* (New York: Aronson, 1978), 127.

3. Mike Mason, *The Mystery of Marriage: As Iron Sharpens Iron* (Portland, Oreg.: Multnomah, 1985), 138.

2

ABDICATING POWER

Eighteen-year-old Hank arrived home from school, tossed his books on the floor, raided the refrigerator, and plopped down in front of the television. He was soon transfixed by MTV, focused on the various heavy metal musicians that shrieked and gyrated on the screen.

"Hello, sweetheart!" his mother Linda beamed at Hank as she hurried into the room, carrying his carefully ironed and folded laundry with her.

He grunted in response.

"How was your day at school?"

Another grunt.

Linda noticed the bag of Doritos® in his lap. "Didn't you find the sandwiches I left in the fridge for you?"

"I hate ham. You know that."

"Oh, Hank. I thought you liked ham!" Linda felt a surge of disappointment. "But I'm making your favorite dinner tonight—tacos. OK?"

She stood watching, waiting for a response. There wasn't one, so she changed the subject. "Hank, honey, some of these shirts are getting a little old, aren't they? Shall we buy you some new ones?"

"Yeah, sure," he mumbled, turning up the volume.

After hanging the shirts in the closet, Linda squeezed Hank's shoulders affectionately. "We'll go shopping Saturday, OK? We'll go to lunch and make a day of it!"

He shrugged. "Whatever. I don't know yet what I'm doing Saturday."

"But honey, don't you want me to buy you some new clothes?"

"Whatever, Mom. By the way, I need you to type a paper tonight." Linda's heart sank. She'd been planning to go out with a friend for dinner that night.

Hank turned up the volume again and leaned forward, pulling away from her hands. Feeling dismissed, Linda tousled her son's hair. "No problem. Just let me know when you're ready for me to do that typing."

Linda picked up the schoolbooks Hank had thrown on the floor, carefully arranging them on his bookshelf. Glancing at him one last time she left the room. Then she phoned her friend and apologetically canceled dinner.

"Hank needs me to type for him," she explained cheerfully. "And you know how important it is for us to be there for our kids. And besides, if my boy's happy, I'm happy too."

Linda depends on Hank for feelings of value and worth. Her personal identity is all wrapped up in being a mother, and so her world revolves around her son. She sacrificially serves him, never counting the cost. No matter how coldly he treats her, how much he takes advantage of her, or how disinterested he is in her, Hank remains the "You" in Linda's life—and dependence is the paradigm of "You":

> ↝ "You need me."
> ↝ "You take care of me."
> ↝ "You make me happy."

There are many reasons for dependence, and different kinds of dependency.

- Emotional dependency means that my sense of worth and security come from your opinion of me.
- Intellectual dependency means that you do my thinking for me.
- Spiritual dependency means that you have the spiritual responsibility for me.
- Physical dependency means that you take care of me.

THREE CORRUPTIONS

Although unaware of it, the dependent, controlled person is using destructive love. By destructive love, we mean a love without power, without a sense of self, without boundaries, and based on an exaggerated need for someone else's approval. This kind of love condones evil and eventually creates agony.

Why would anyone choose to be so helpless? The goal of dependent people is to avoid pain and to maintain peace at any cost. They prefer to live in a world of denial rather than to confront reality. They are driven by their desire to prevent conflict.

And what happens to the person who chooses to be dependent? First of all, the dependent person ends up corrupted—corrupted in three separate ways.

THE DENIAL OF REALITY

The first of these corruptions is denial. Denial corrupts. It is the refusal to face the truth—reality—clearly a form of dishonesty.

Timmen L. Cermak says, "Denial stems from an internal preoccupation with avoiding pain. It is like a flashlight that works in reverse, casting shadows rather than light. It throws darkness over selected parts of the world to make them less noticeable, enabling us to hide embarrassing parts of our personality from our own vision, even though these parts may be obvious to everyone else . . . Denial prevents us from seeing things that make us too uncomfortable."[1]

The three rules that are central to every dysfunctional family were coined by Claudia Black: "Don't talk, don't trust, don't feel."[2] We not only keep the truth of our reality from others, we don't even admit it to ourselves. We ignore our rage, shame, anger, pain, and rejection and we shower others with the love we need but would never risk asking for. In fact we become so adept at denying our own reality (Daddy's not really being violent—he's just tired), that we see only what we want to in our dating relationships, workplaces, churches, and partners. We simply deny the rest.

Curiously, although we are not in touch with our own feelings of fear, anger, and other negative emotions, we become adept at figuring out what others are feeling and what everybody else should do. When we become embroiled in their chaos and crises, we are too busy to face our own character deficits, disappointment about past and present relationships, emptiness, and aloneness. Blind to ourselves, we become emotionally paralyzed, easily influenced, and quick to adopt anything that makes us feel good.

THE WORSHIP OF FALSE GODS

Not only are dependents corrupted by denial, they are corrupted by idolatry. Self-hatred, self-contempt, and self-neglect can cause us to become approval junkies. "I will do anything to get your approval—my worth and happiness lie outside of me and in you." When that happens, the person who is supposed to give us our approval becomes our god, essentially taking on the role of an idol—our higher power. We are so totally dependent on that person that we cannot leave or separate ourselves from the relationship. As a result, we are unable to set limits with them. We need them. Without them we feel an inner void.

Diane was wildly in love with her husband, Dan. And Dan was wildly in love with himself. He was particularly proud of his sexual prowess and even bragged to his wife about affairs he had had with several women at work.

Pretty and timid, Diane was heartsick over these "flings," as he called them, but managed to take them in stride. She knew what she had to do—become a better wife. She took gourmet cooking classes. Attended sexual-awareness seminars. Lost weight. Told Dan he was wonderful. Bought him presents.

But the more she did, the more abusive and unkind he became. His irresponsibility increased. He told Diane she disgusted him, even though he couldn't quite explain why.

Finally he moved out, leaving her for a single man's lifestyle. Diane began therapy—she had no idea who she was, what she liked, or what she wanted in life. She had become "the perfect wife" for Dan but had lost herself in the process. Now she had to start all over again.

Although the dependent person suffers from low self-esteem, at the same time she (or he) may also treasure an inflated sense of importance. She believes that she can fix everyone and handle anything.

Dependents become rescuers and attempt to save people from the consequences of their own choices. They do this by acting when they should let go, or by failing to act when they really should. (In Alcoholics Anonymous-type programs, these people are sometimes called *enablers.*) Worse, they become caretakers, doing for another what he is capable of doing for himself. The hope is that the catered-to individual will learn to love them, appreciate what they are doing, and reciprocate in kind.

THE ACCEPTANCE OF EVIL

Another corrupting quality in dependence is the condoning of evil—in fact, the enabling of another to do evil. Because of a false belief that "love means that I don't make waves and that I don't confront," the dependent person puts up with the abuse of people and substances. Because of an exaggerated terror of conflict, rejection, or being alone, the dependent person puts up with any evil without comment or complaint. If a potential confrontation threatens, it is more comfortable for him to withdraw than to speak up.

WHAT DEPENDENTS BELIEVE

Besides being corrupted by their behavior, dependents also experience other negative consequences. They are so terrified at the possibility of rejection and the threat of not being needed that they will not risk diversity of thought. Soon they find themselves accepted for their "yes" responses. Their belief system, which keeps them from rocking the boat, looks something like this:

- I am totally responsible for other people's feelings and actions.
- I am the cause of other people's problems and therefore must bail them out.
- I must meet every need and answer every cry for help.
- I am defined by the people I am in relationship with.
- I live at the mercy of other people's demands and expectations.
- I have no right to privacy, plans, or personal well-being.
- I have no choice in my relationships.
- I have an insatiable need to be admired.
- I am hopelessly flawed and unchangeable.
- I am motivated by fear and guilt.
- I am to save others from the negative consequences of their choices.
- I do things for people that they could and should do for themselves.
- I must never say no.

WEARING MANY MASKS

The dependent lives in an others-centered world and often confuses love with pity. If we are dependents, we are drawn to those who seem to need us in some way. We virtually invite them to use us. These individuals may be unable to relate to others. They may be cold, unaffectionate, or stubborn. Quite possibly they are selfish, sulking, or melancholy. The persons we are attracted to may be irresponsible or unable to commit or be faithful. We may even discover that they have never been able to love anyone.

But does any of this stop us? Of course not.

If someone needs us, it is a sign that the relationship was "meant to be" in our lives—a godsend, so to speak. God has surely called us to "minister" to their needs. Worse yet, if we happen to find ourselves in a male-female relationship, "it must be love!"

Meanwhile, although we throw ourselves headlong into these rescuing situations, we may at the same time distance and isolate ourselves from others. Dependents are passionately committed to never being hurt again, a passion that demonstrates itself in tremendous self-sufficiency. We do things like listening for hours while others pour out their troubles, but we never risk vulnerability ourselves.

We often continue to wear the masks that we learned to hide behind in childhood, rather than facing our pain and our feelings of being out of control.

Perhaps we had to be "perfect" in order to be accepted. Now we spend every waking moment trying to discover what is expected of us so we can react appropriately—beyond the possibility of criticism. Like little turtles we pull our heads in and don't risk ever exposing our pain and imperfections. And all the while we keep telling ourselves that we don't need others and that we can handle everything ourselves.

Dependents isolate themselves because they feel that in receiving from others, they ruin their chances of truly being loved.

The dependent tries to keep things predictable and secure. He masks his efforts to control people and situations as being "helpful."

Those of us who have been raised in homes in which no one was emotionally or physically available for us mistrust the family environment. For us it was a source of pain, danger, and harm rather than a haven of safety, security, and stability. We were so overwhelmed by our adversities there that we now

choose to be "on duty" for others. We do this to protect ourselves from the absolute panic that wells up in our soul when
we are at the mercy of someone else.

THE DANGERS OF INTIMACY

Dan came to us for help because he was always feeling
guilty. First of all, he couldn't bear it when a friend became
angry with him. He would do anything to appease anybody. His
basic assumption was that he was responsible for everyone
else's feelings. As a result, he was like a chameleon that
changes its colors to suit every occasion.

Dan had no idea where he ended and others began. He
was defined only by the people to whom he was relating. He
was willing to accept more than 50 percent of the responsibility, guilt, and blame in all relationships—quite an expert at
"bearing the burden." He felt selfish when he said no. So Dan
always said yes.

Like Dan, the dependent person has no concept of boundaries. He has lost his sense of self. He is unable to determine
where his responsibility begins and where it ends. Before long,
he has become a jellyfish with no backbone. No one knows
how he feels, what he thinks, or what makes him tick. He—like
other dependents—has blocked out the possibility of intimacy.
Why?

- Intimacy involves a willingness to trust others, but dependents only trust themselves.
- Intimacy involves honesty and self-definition, but dependents change in response to the persons they are with.
- Intimacy involves vulnerability, but dependents know everyone else at the same time no one knows them.
- Intimacy involves risk, but dependents don't want to be
hurt—only to be needed.

Because of these attitudes, dependents are not able to be
real, to give or receive love, or to offer forgiveness to themselves or anyone else.

WHAT'S TO BE GAINED?

FINDING A CARETAKER

In light of all this, what would cause anyone to remain in the controlled, or dependent, position? An obvious reason is a desire to be cared for. Perhaps an employee sees job security in his sycophantic behavior.

A son may feel that by being dependent on his parents, all his needs will be met without a great deal of effort on his part.

In marriage, a woman may expect her husband to be her "sugar daddy." He is to take care of her in the comfortable manner she's forever dreamed about. Maybe he is to be the father she always wanted. In her mind, when he marries her he will have signed, sealed, and delivered an entirely satisfactory contract. Henceforth, she will never have to work. She will never have to bother herself with financial details. Best of all, she will never have to grow up.

In the same sense, some men entering holy wedlock expect to slip easily from one mother to the next. The wife's most important job is to take care of hubby and to make him happy. As a "good wife" she is to clean, cook, comfort, nurture, soothe, admire, encourage, listen, sympathize, and support.

Needless to say, when both individuals are looking for a caretaker, it's not surprising to find both their conflicts registering on the Richter scale.

RECAPTURING A LOST LOVE

Another reason men and women remain dependent is because of a troubled family background. As children, they got a taste of love. Momentarily they basked in the glow of love and adoration. Then, suddenly and perhaps without explanation, the source of love vanished physically, emotionally, or both.

When these children mature, their desire is to recapture the joy of lost love. They yearn to merge with a safe, nurturing person with whom there will be no differences, conflicts, distinctions, or boundaries. In this fantasy, they believe that the person they long for will never deny them anything.

How well does this work? We might say, "The rocks in his head will fill the holes in hers." A desperate individual such as this will attract needy, controlling people like a magnet. Still, that may seem preferable to the terror and emptiness of being emotionally abandoned.

The most dangerous words a dependent can say are "Oh, it won't be so bad. I can make it work. Love changes everything." We choose to believe the deadly myth that we can "fix" other people. All they need is our tender, loving care. Nothing is too much trouble, takes too much time, or is too costly if it will "help" somebody else. This kind of thinking, by the way, could be the embodiment of a childhood wish: "I wish I could fix my parents by being more loving."

Some people actually become addicted to difficult relationships. The highs and lows and the adrenaline rush of the good times keep them trudging through the awfulness. Addictions—whether to substances, habits, or people—temporarily relieve our pain. Addictive substances distract us and detract from our ability to deal with many aspects of life. In a similar way, pain, emptiness, fear, shame, and anger can be avoided by taking someone on as a personal project. Willingly we place ourselves in a position of dependency. We need to be needed. Without a relationship to be obsessed with, we may actually find ourselves in a state of withdrawal, with all its accompanying symptoms.

COMPENSATING FOR PERSONAL FLAWS
AND A FEELING OF UNWORTHINESS

Low self-esteem has a great deal to do with dependent behavior. When a child has been verbally or physically attacked, shamed in public, or made to feel that he is "bad" in some way, he accepts the blame for anything and everything that goes wrong. This child believes that he or she doesn't deserve to love and be loved simply for "being." Instead he believes that he can only be loved for what he does. He feels flawed, and the only way to escape this reality is to do good works in order to compensate. Guilt feelings abound, along with the vague fear that hidden flaws will eventually be discovered. He struggles to be perfect, because he thinks that if he isn't perfect, he isn't worth loving.

As children like this mature, they often experience a loneliness and isolation for which they silently berate themselves. They hurl words of self-indictment and self-punishment against themselves, becoming their own worst enemies. They may unconsciously sabotage love relationships and career opportunities that come their way, feeling unworthy of success. There is little need for Satan, "the accuser of the brethren," to be bothered with these individuals. His work is made easy by their own self-condemnation.

Our need to punish ourselves keeps us stuck in the dependent position. Many of us have a very low opinion of ourselves. When bad things come our way, we decide that we deserve them.

For Christians, this can be an insidious form of rebellion, a resistance to grace. It amounts to believing that if I can punish myself enough, or can get someone else to punish me for my sins, mistakes, and failures, then the resulting guilt will help me feel as though I am paying penance—earning my own salvation, so to speak.

When we usurp God's authority and refuse to accept His unconditional love and grace, we set ourselves above Him. This is a dangerous form of idolatry. "They exchanged the truth of God for a lie, and worshiped and served created things rather than the Creator—who is forever praised, Amen" (Romans 1:25).

RECREATING THE PAST

As boys and girls, we all experienced a very real sense of dependence in a world of bigger, more powerful people. If childhood was painful, we may have promised ourselves that when we grew up, things would be different.

Unfortunately, as adults, men and women who have come from unhappy family backgrounds have a strong tendency to choose a familiar badness over unfamiliar goodness. Kindness, gentleness, consideration, and compliments don't "feel right." Instead we end up duplicating childhood situations and relationships. This is reflected in the fact that divorced people often marry the same type of person again and again.

Additionally, there is a drive within many of us to recreate our childhood families and try to make them come out better— rewriting the script with a happy ending, so to speak. In doing so, we respond deeply to the familiar type of emotionally unavailable individuals we know so well, subconsciously believing that we can transform them through our love. We are simply not attracted to healthy people who can give us what we need. They make us feel uncomfortable. We've never known anyone but abusive people.

We may be afraid of the unpredictability of people we can't control, people who might leave us. But Scripture takes a dim view of this sort of repetition compulsion. Continually repeating our errors is like a dog returning "to its own vomit," Proverbs says (26:11)

Sometimes we try to recreate the past even when it isn't there. William Gaylin says that "if we experienced something too strongly in the past, we may anticipate it where we ought not and perceive it where it does not exist. If, for example, we were intimidated by a punitive father who terrified us, we may approach all authority figures with the bias of that early dominant memory. The memory of that authority may possess a greater reality to us than the actual authority with whom we were involved. Regardless of how gentle and unchallenging the authority figure is, we may approach each teacher, each employer as though he had both the power and the personality of the dominant father who once ruled our life."[3]

PLAYING THE MARTYR ROLE

Sometimes the controlled person stays in the dependent role because he enjoys playing the role of a victim or martyr. The victim always externalizes his troubles onto the abuser. All his problems therefore become the other person's fault.

- "If only I hadn't married Jim"
- "If only I didn't have my stupid boss"
- "If only I didn't have to put up with Sophie"
- "If only my husband were a better Christian"

The implication is that if others would change, all would be well. The martyr externalizes all responsibility, blame, and fault. In so doing, he takes on a morally superior, judgmental position.

LIKE MOTHER, LIKE DAUGHTER

Sometimes a woman stays in a dependent position as an unconscious "oath of fidelity" to her own mother.[4] In families where the marital relationship was destructive, the controlling father may have blocked the mother from pursuing her own dreams. It is not unusual to find that daughters from these marriages manifest passive and dependent behavior. They view their own separateness and autonomy as disloyalty or betrayal of their mothers.

In a similar vein, if the mother was an abused wife the daughter may assume that dependency is the only safe stance she can take in a close relationship.

Perhaps a young girl has witnessed screaming matches, black eyes, her mother's being thrown into walls and through windows, hair being pulled, and knives being used as weapons. She may even have observed rape or other sexual abuse. By submitting to continuous abuse, the mother is telling the daughter nonverbally that she can't survive without a man, no matter how destructive that man might be.

Some daughters have come to believe that men have all the power in relationships and women don't have any. They've concluded that no matter what a man does to a woman, she's powerless to protect herself. And, of course, they are convinced that, in spite of everything, a woman simply can't exist without a man.

SPIRITUAL AND CULTURAL EXCUSES

SPIRITUAL PASSIVITY

Passivity can keep us stuck in the dependent position. And Christian passivity can sound so very spiritual. "Oh, I'm just waiting on the Lord. . . . I don't want to get ahead of His perfect timing, you know." In reality, what these words often mean is, "I'm afraid of risking, of being hurt again, of putting myself out there. . . . I'm *not* willing to initiate any communication, any action, any plan even though I'm needy, lonely, and miserable."

With spiritual passivity may also come an unconscious belief that we must remain in a position of weakness in order for our most important relationships to survive. If God has put us in subjection to someone, won't He punish us if we speak up?

CULTURAL PRESSURE

Cultural forces also keep women from being aware of their own strength. Traditional messages reinforce the belief that women need men to take care of them. After all, aren't women highly emotional, indecisive, illogical, and manipulative with little control over their lives (besides having PMS!)? By contrast are not men stronger, more competent, logical, decisive, rational, in control, and generally smarter than women?

We love Harriet Goldhor Lerner's assessment: "The message is that the weaker sex must protect the stronger sex from recognizing the strength of the weaker sex lest the stronger sex feels weakened by the strength of the weaker sex."[5]

Lerner goes on to say that women learn that being an autonomous person hurts other people, especially men. Women are expected to sacrifice important parts of themselves in order to remain in important relationships. Culture often reinforces the messages daughters learned in their families: "You won't be loved if you become too independent and too successful."

TOO SCARED TO BE ANGRY

Fear of our own negative emotions may keep us stuck. A child raised in a controlling environment learns very quickly that his (or her) feelings don't matter. In fact she is not supposed to feel. She is to deny her feelings, especially feelings of anger, and is simply to "love" the father or mother who is acting in an abusive manner.

Conflict in childhood may have resulted in physical and/or emotional abuse. If your opinion has never been validated and valued, or worse yet, has been mocked or even attacked, it is no wonder that you shy away from conflict. Often children become so effective at submerging their anger that they become overcompliant, overadaptive, and oversubmissive. The problem is that the more we deny our feelings and needs, the angrier we become. If our method for dealing with anger is compliance, we become an explosion waiting to happen.

Anger is a normal, God-given human emotion. Its purpose is to tell us that danger is coming our way. Yet some Christians believe that it is a sin to be angry. "Peace at any cost" is their motto. The final result is an extremely angry person putting on a "happy-face" that says "I am not angry!" What a breeding ground this provides for passive-aggressive behavior.

SUBMISSION OR SUBMERSION?

A misunderstanding of submission can also keep a woman stuck in the dependent position. (More about marital submission in the next chapter.) Submission, falsely defined, has imprisoned many a woman for a lifetime. Unless she discovers the truth of the matter, she may never become the woman God created her to be.

One of our client's voiced her dissatisfaction with this arrangement in a most creative letter:

> False Submission
> 1 Dependent Woman Lane
> Lost Autonomy, Land of False Guilt 11111
>
> Dear husband who believes in false submission,
>
> I have been living in this fantasy world with you for over twelve years now. For your sake I gave up my freedom, my personal life goals, and my personhood. I thought that by doing this I would be pleasing God and you.
>
> I have allowed you to rob me of my identity, and I feel very angry about this. I have allowed you to strip me of my personal dignity and self-worth. I have hidden my talents and intelligence. You have not allowed me a voice or an opinion in this relationship.
>
> While I know it will not happen overnight, with God's help, day by day, I am going to move out of this address. I want to learn to relate to you as a woman with *this* address:
>
> > 1 Wholeness Square
> > Interdependent, Evergrowing Place 222
> >
> > With Love,
> >
> > Your wife

What had this woman's life been like? She was married to a Christian "rageaholic," and was never certain what would spark his wrath. If the anger struck while her husband was at the table, the result was always the same. He would pick up the ketchup bottle and heave it at the wall. The result left the kitchen looking like a war zone. As a godly, "submissive" Christian wife she was to leave the table and clean up the mess without comment. He would continue eating as if nothing had happened. She obeyed for twenty-five years. He never changed. And he seemed like such a nice guy when they met.

Some people find themselves in the dependent position in relationships because they have a poor ability to judge character. Never having been in a relationship with a safe person, they don't have a clue about what a safe person acts like. The book of Proverbs says that one of the jobs of a father is to teach a child to be discriminating in his choices. If our parents were unable to enlighten us because they didn't know, we are necessarily uninformed. (To learn more about what a safe person is like, read on.)

TAKING A LOOK AT OURSELVES

Meanwhile, see how you respond to the following "dependent" checklist:

1. I find that my need to be liked is greater than my need to be honest.
2. I feel that solving another's problems or reliving his/her pain is extremely important—no matter what the emotional cost to me.
3. I find that the quality of my life is determined by the quality of the people around me.
4. I realize that my good feelings depend on approval from other people in my life.
5. I have a difficult time saying no.
6. I feel powerless to change myself or my situation.
7. I protect those close to me from the consequences of their behavior. I lie for them, cover up for them, and never let others say anything derogatory about them.
8. I feel used, taken advantage of, resentful, and retaliatory much of the time.

9. I am certain that I would be helpless if something happened to my spouse (boyfriend/girlfriend).
10. I have a difficult time making decisions.
11. I feel better about myself when I solve other people's problems.
12. I will do anything to avoid another person's rejection.
13. I will do anything to avoid another person's anger.
14. My own interests, wants, and hobbies have been put on a shelf. My time is consumed with my significant other's wants, interests, and hobbies.
15. I believe that my significant other is a reflection of me.
16. I experience much more passion in a relationship that is stormy and full of drama.
17. I want everything to be perfect, and I blame myself when anything goes wrong.
18. I have a difficult time identifying and expressing my own feelings.
19. I pretend that everything is fine when it isn't.
20. The struggle to get others to love and accept me dominates my life.

NOBODY'S PERFECT

It is important to note that every individual is different. Some dependents are not trying to change their controller as much as they are just trying to survive. Others are attempting to respect scriptural injunctions. Most of us, whether we are controllers or dependents, have simply not yet learned a better way to live. The Scriptures (Matthew 7:1–5) put it this way: "Do not judge, or you too will be judged. For in the same way you judge others, you will be judged, and with the measure you use, it will be measured to you.

"Why do you look at the speck of sawdust in your brother's eye and pay no attention to the plank in your own eye? How can you say to your brother 'Let me take the speck out of your eye' when all the time there is a plank in your own eye? You hypocrite, first take the plank out of your own eye, and then you will see clearly to remove the speck from your brother's eye."

With these words in mind, I must always remember that I am unqualified to to sit in judgment of someone else's use of either destructive power or destructive love, because I have no idea what pain in his past has led him to hide in such a way. Hurt people always hurt people. Perhaps I also have neglected to examine or even acknowledge my own tendencies toward toxic forms of control and love. We all slip in and out of these behaviors throughout our lives until we really learn the "more excellent way."

As you will quickly see from the chart below, there is no "better" role between dominators and dependents. In fact, their motivations are uncannily similar.

Controlling Person Dominating	Controlled Person Dependent

1. Ends up corrupted
   a. becomes a law unto himself
   b. pride and power corrupt
   c. truth is misrepresented or denied
   d. selfishness corrupts
	1. Ends up corrupted
	   a. denial corrupts
	   b. idolatry corrupts
	   c. omnipotence corrupts
	   d. condoning and enabling evil corrupts

2. Is so convinced of his/her rightness that he/she cannot tolerate diversity of thought	2. Is so terrified of rejection and not being needed that he/she cannot tolerate diversity of thought
3. Lives in a black and white world involving dichotomous thinking	3. Lives in an other-centered fantasy world
4. Distances and isolates from others	4. Distances and isolates from others even when clinging

5. Tries to keep things predictable and will do anything covertly or overtly to keep reality from changing	5. Tries to keep things predictable and secure by being "helpful"
6. Has no concept of boundaries	6. Has no concept of boundaries
7. Blocks the possibility for intimacy by destroying integrity, trust, and dialogue	7. Blocks the possibility of intimacy by destroying integrity, trust, and dialogue
8. Becomes his/her own higher power	8. Makes the other person his/her higher power

ICEBERGS AND ISLANDS

Each of us is much like a gigantic iceberg. When we first ask Jesus to be our personal Savior, we acknowledge that we are in a state of emotional and spiritual chaos. Yet despite our confusion, many of us still believe that God is pretty lucky to have us. Surely He won't have as much work to do on us as with some other people we could mention.

And so when we begin our relationship with Jesus, each of us gives Him a surface gift—the gift of our "perfect, ideal self." Jesus gladly takes our gift, but He knows what we're often reluctant to admit—that this gift represents only the tip of the iceberg.

During World War II battles were fought in the Pacific Ocean over small islands along the Asian coast. When the first marines or sailors landed on the shore the American flag was raised, establishing the American presence there—a beachhead had been taken. There still might be hundreds, even thousands, of enemy troops on the island. They would eventually have to be defeated. But even before their demise, the marines would radio back that the island was captured.

In the same way, even though we already belong to Jesus, He wants us to get to know ourselves deeply. That involves fighting darkness, seeking illumination as David did when he wrote, "Search me O God and know my heart; test me and know my anxious thoughts. See if there is any offensive way in me, and lead me in the way everlasting" (Psalm 139: 23–24).

David was admitting that he didn't really know what was in his own heart. And neither do we. But with God's help and gentle guidance, we can get to know ourselves more deeply. Naturally He accepts the facades—the shiny, attractive, positive, sweet-smelling, competent, ideal, politically correct masks we wear. He realizes how little self-knowledge we have and therefore how foolish we can sometimes be. How He longs for us to give Him our hurt, pain, anger, fear, guilt, bitterness, self-reliance, blocked memories, dishonesty, shame, failures, insecurities, lust, and self-pity.

In short, Jesus wants us to know about the submerged part of our icebergs, the unconquered territory of our islands. He wants us to own them and to offer them to Him. That way, whether we are loveless power mongers or powerless lovers, we can begin to move toward a healthier way of relating to one another. Our Lord wants to lead us into a Christ-like, powerfully loving, brand-new way of life. And not a minute too soon, we might add.

FINDING TRUE EQUALITY

One of the most typical comments made by struggling individuals is "Things will get better. I just need to be more patient." Sometimes they comfort themselves with the Scripture "Weeping may remain for a night, but rejoicing comes in the morning" (Psalm 30:5). This is indeed an encouraging promise from God, and anyone who suffers does well to hold it close to his heart. But it brings to mind an interesting story.

An old rabbi posed a question one day, "Children, how can we determine the moment of dawn, when the night ends and the day begins?"

One listener ventured forth, "When I see the difference between a dog and a sheep?"

"No," replied the rabbi.

Another listener tried. "Is it when I can see the difference between a fig tree and a grape vine?"

"No," said the rabbi, shaking his head.

"Please tell us the answer," his audience asked.

The old man smiled. "You know when the night ends and the day begins when you can look into the face of *any human* being and have enough light to recognize that person as your brother or your sister. It is when you can say 'I can see myself in you.' Up until that time it is night, and the darkness is still with us."

In order to develop healthy, interdependent relationships, we must stop saying things like:

"I am superior to you."
"I am beneath you and worship you."
"I am an extension of you."
"I am in control of you."
"I am responsible for you."
"I am utterly absorbed by you."
"I am longing to see change in you."

It is when we can say, "I see myself in you—my equal, my co-laborer, my brother or sister in Christ," that the night truly ends and the morning dawns. Only then can our tears begin to be dried.

Notes

1. Timmen L. Cermak, *A Time to Heal* (Los Angeles, Calif.: Jeremy P. Tarcher, 1988), 33–34.
2. Claudia Black, *It Will Never Happen to Me* (Denver: M.A.C. Printing, 1982), 31–49.
3. Willard Gaylin, *Feelings* (New York: Harper & Row, 1979), 22–23.
4. Harriet Goldhor Lerner, *Women in Therapy* (New York: Harper & Row, 1989), 163.
5. Ibid., 163.

3

THE POWER OF LOVE

S ara, an attractive redhead, had worked for fifteen years as George's personal assistant. She was a shy, quiet woman who rarely expressed her opinion to anyone, least of all to George. Meanwhile, highly successful and wealthy, George was very dependent on her to implement his sometimes impractical ideas and to cover for him when he wasn't able to keep his promises.

Sara privately loathed George's business style. He could be compassionate and warm one minute, curt and cold the next. Most of the time he was an unbearable tyrant. He also had a tendency to generously offer people the moon, only to forget everything he'd said five minutes later. Letters invariably arrived from disappointed and disgruntled clients and colleagues, which George automatically handed to Sara. "Answer this, will you? Say whatever you want. I don't care what you tell him."

Sara had become very creative in making up excuses to explain George's forgetfulness, irritability, and dishonesty.

Although Sara never said a word to George about her disapproval, she had her own ways of handling things. Over the years she had efficiently and tidily organized George's business in such a way that she had become completely indispensable to him. She was the only one who handled George's contracts, finances, and appointment schedules, and she was the only one who could legally cosign company checks. Meanwhile, she compliantly sympathized with George, made sure his favorite coffee was available to him, ran his errands, and listened to his marital problems.

And, for extra measure, Sara had a long-standing sexual relationship with George, in which she participated without demands or complaints. Because of his frequent explosions and exploitation of others, she had long ago lost all feeling for him, yet she continued to act out a lover's role. After all, it assured her of a prestigious position, a paycheck, and an extra measure of personal control—just in case she ever needed it.

Of course, when Sara allowed the truth to linger in her mind, she hated herself for what she was doing—she felt like a prostitute. And although George's wife was distant and difficult, he never could quite accept his own ongoing adultery. Only by staying obsessively busy did Sara and George avoid facing their predicament.

This miserable man and woman identified themselves as Christian believers. They resented each other bitterly and were repulsed by their own behavior. Each was dependent in one way and controlling in another. But neither of them was willing to break their sick cycle.

In all areas of relationship, people tend to polarize between the extremes of love and power—and either extreme is destructive.

Loveless power leads to manipulation, control, domination, and broken relationships. It demands subservience, destroys trust, blocks communication, denies truth, undermines self-esteem, and destroys integrity.

Powerless love, on the other hand, leads to a weak sentimentality, permissiveness, denial of the truth, and—ultimately—codependency.

LOVELESS POWER	POWERFUL LOVE	POWERLESS LOVE
(controller)	(Christ-like)	(controlled)

A POWERFUL LOVE

The Scripture introduces us to a powerful description of *love* and a loving description of *power* in the person of Jesus Christ. His integration of these two principles of relationship brought restoration to relationships that had been destroyed by the overemphasis on power or the overemphasis on love.

Second Timothy 1:7 says, "God did not give us a spirit of timidity, but a spirit of power, of love and of self-discipline." If we're afraid, our fear certainly doesn't come from God. It is the result of our experiences in our families, our past, our culture, and our churches. And what is it we fear in relationships? We find that it usually has to do with absorption (the loss of uniqueness), abandonment (the loss of belonging), exposure (the loss of dignity), and attack (the loss of safety). Sometimes we also fear financial, material, or social loss.

WEARING TWO HATS

After reading chapters 1 and 2, you have no doubt identified yourself as exhibiting extremes of loveless power or powerless love. But have you noticed that in certain relational settings you seem to be living paradoxically? Sara and George certainly were—they went back and forth between dependence and control many times each day. In a different way, Ruth discovered that she was also both controller and controlled.

Ruth is a corporate executive. Beautifully dressed and manicured, she makes a powerful impression wherever she goes. And her employees genuinely love her. Besides being a generous and gracious manager, she is articulate, independent, and decisive.

Because of her strategic position in the corporation, Ruth is frequently called upon to resolve conflicts, and she does so with great finesse. She is well paid, well suited for her job, and well respected.

Then she goes home and Jeremy, her boyfriend, shows up.

Suddenly Ruth is in a dependent position. He makes all the decisions in a relationship that completely revolves around him. As far as Jeremy is concerned, Ruth either keeps the ground rules he's set, or she's out of his life. He's made this clear to her in no uncertain terms. She does his laundry, cooks his meals, meets his sexual needs, and allows him to use her platinum American Express card whether he pays his part of the bill or not. Even though she can't quite seem to please Jeremy, she can't imagine living without him, either.

Ruth has begun therapy because she is experiencing a debilitating depression and can't understand why.

Whether relationships involve parents and children, dating couples, employers and employees, friends, or husbands and wives, there are at least three different stages relationships go through.

Stage 1: The Unhealthy Hierarchy

> A. Heavenly Hierarchy
> "I want whatever you want, dear."

> B. Hellish Hierarchy
> "I can't live with you, and yet I can't live without you."

Stage 2: The Isolate Relationship

> A. Reactive Isolation
> "I live in opposition to you. I will tell you who you should be."

> B. Required Individuation
> "I don't care what you do. I need to discover who I am."

Stage 3: The Healthy Partnership

> A. Hesitant Interaction
> "I want to tell you who I am, and I want to get to know you."

> B. Healthy Interdependence
> "I love being in relationship with you. I love the challenge of it. I am capable of living alone. But what companionship, what fun, and what growth would be lacking in my life!"

Since marriage is usually the most challenging of all relationships, and since we've had to work our own way through
these stages of relationship, we'd like to share with you some
highlights and low points from our own journey.

A MARRIAGE JOURNEY

THE UNHEALTHY HIERARCHY

Early in our marriage, while we still had stars in our eyes,
we received some strong and convincing teaching about the
marriage relationship. Both of us were committed Christians,
we really loved each other, and we wanted to make our marriage a great one according to God's standards.

We were taught that in the biblical Christian relationship,
the husband serves God, and the wife serves her husband. Today we call this style of marriage the "unhealthy hierarchy." We
also call it unbiblical—it reflects a twisted interpretation of
Scripture. At that time in our lives, however, we swallowed this
teaching hook, line, and sinker.

The idea is that the husband is free to do whatever he
wants, and it is assumed that whatever he wants to do is God's
will because God has placed him in authority. Meanwhile, the
wife is to be totally dedicated to the care and feeding of her
husband—and his ego. She will become a "Revised Standard
Version" of her husband, almost a clone, if she is truly a submissive wife. Any conflicts that arise are intolerable. Undoubt-
edly they signal a rebellious attitude on the part of the wife.

In those early days of marriage, the Christianity we sub-
scribed to required pretenses and masks. It did not acknowledge pain and reality. Image was more important than integrity;
externals more significant than internals. Women in particular
were taught—indirectly of course—to conceal their attempts to
control rather than to confess their needs.

At one wedding we attended the pastor addressed the
young couple with these words: "You are to be involved in a
partnership marriage." Then he turned to the groom and in-

structed, "You will be the head partner." Next, he addressed the bride: "And you, my dear, will be the silent partner."

This teaching pressures women to hide aspects of themselves so they won't displease or upset their husbands. It isn't long until they feel that they are inferior and inadequate. Soon they have not only dropped their names but have also lost their identity.

Perhaps you've observed young women who are radiant with hope and anticipation on their wedding day. Three years later, there is a dullness in their eyes, a shyness and insecurity you've never noticed before. They are lacking confidence, and often they have lost the love they once felt for the man they married. Whether they know it or not, they feel that their need for their husbands is much greater than their husbands' need for them.

When this unhealthy hierarchy involves a man who has an enormous need to control, we call him a "married bachelor."

I (Dave) never meant to become a married bachelor, yet that's exactly what I was. I didn't fit the picture of the macho, controlling husband, but I just expected Jan never to disagree, always to be there for me, and always to make my life as comfortable and conflict-free as possible. I felt we could have a wonderful marriage if she would just cooperate.

Fresh out of seminary, I wanted to prove myself in my first pastorate. My responsibilities at the church kept me at the beck and call of people six nights a week. Soon my life was revolving around my ministry.

One day I was standing in front of forty couples, leading a marriage retreat, expounding the chain of marital authority. A mere thirty minutes later, in the privacy of our room, Jan was yanking the wedding ring off her finger and throwing it at me. It missed, but the scene that followed had an impact all its own.

"I've had it! I can't stand being married!" Jan yelled at me. "This is no way for a human being to live. You've been doing your thing for years in our relationship and actually spiritualizing it. Now it's my turn."

What in the world had happened to the Perfect Christian Couple? As a minister's wife, I (Jan) had spent a great deal of time studying the faces in our congregation. I liked the people but didn't feel that they knew me. When I was with them, I was the pastor's wife, Dave's clone. The only place where I felt people really knew me was at the college where I was teaching.

THE ISOLATE RELATIONSHIP

On that fateful day at the retreat, I stopped being a dependent woman whose entire life was built around Dave. Up until then, he had been my god. I lived reacting to his needs—my life was consumed with trying to meet them. Dave was unaware of the impact his behavior was having on me. I longed to be nurtured, but when he did special things for me, I questioned and devalued everything—I even read his kindness as being manipulative. What did he want from me? Did he have an ulterior motive?

Both of us were terrified of both abandonment and engulfment. Gradually, my "underground" movement against Dave's control went from covert to overt. That's when we entered a new stage, which we now call an "isolate relationship."

At that point, I made the decision to rebuild my life around myself and my career as a college instructor. With that resolution came the birth of a two-headed monster that was to cause suffering for both of us.

During that period in our marriage we lived in isolation from each other. Instead of Dave's being the center of my world, my career became central. Dave's career had been central since we were married, so now the battle of the two-headed monster began in earnest, bringing with it distance, loneliness, lack of sensitivity, power struggles, and unmet needs. I threw myself into an ever-increasing effort to define my own identity, inwardly fluctuating between anger and guilt. Meanwhile, Dave felt bewildered, threatened, and betrayed. He attempted to maintain our oneness with controlling behavior. Other spouses sometimes use clinging to accomplish the same.

Although in reality we were emotionally divorced, actual divorce was not an option for us. When we got married, we had committed ourselves to each other for life. So the decision then was not whether or not we'd stay together. It was to decide what kind of life we wanted to have together. How thankful we are now that we were permanently linked for better or worse. Without that vow, we would surely have fled in the midst of the worst and would never have found out how good the best could be.

Eight years passed. In order for Dave to work toward a doctorate in psychology and theology, we made the decision together to relocate in southern California.

We were both happy with this new development. We loved our new home, and I found a teaching position at Biola College that would allow me to continue my career and provide much-needed funds. Then the United States Immigration and Naturalization Service entered the scene. We were Canadians. As such, Dave could study on a student visa but I was not permitted to hold a job. I would have to quit working.

We were faced with the financial reality of paying school tuition, house payments, and food costs without my income. But there was another problem, too. During the first few years of our marriage, my identity had come from being Dave's wife. Then, in total frustration, I had rejected that option and had chosen to base my identity on my career. Now who would I be?

There followed months of depression and agony as I attempted to be superwoman, desperate to prove to the world that I was worth something. It was an emotionally agonizing time. And my career loss was not only my growing edge—it was also to become Dave's.

We began to realize that as long as we'd been husband and wife, our god had been either ourselves or our spouse. This idolatry had warped our relationship with each other. It had also blocked our relationship with each other and with God.

REQUIRED INDIVIDUATION

During those years we had few skills to help us manage our relationship, and we were always shocked to find ourselves acting like our parents in ways we'd vowed we never would. We began to explore the past. What had made us the way we were? Gradually we both became cognizant of our controlling behavior, whether it was covert or overt, and we stopped denying it.

We finally had to acknowledge our controlling as the sin disease it was. We had to take ourselves off the throne and commit ourselves to the lordship of Christ. Jan had to learn that her emptiness was not Dave's fault. He wasn't able to make her happy. We both learned about boundaries, and we discovered that our personal happiness was our own responsibility. We had proved all too well that we couldn't make each other happy, no matter how we tried.

THE HEALTHY PARTNERSHIP

Many nights we talked into the wee hours. We eventually came to see that we had been building our lives on faulty foundations. We could have lived the rest of our married life spiritually and emotionally distant from one another, but we chose to face our pain and restructure the foundations upon which we were building our marriage.

It wasn't easy then, and it isn't easy now. But today we are continuing to learn about our personal ability to give and receive. We've discovered that the replacement for controlling each other is the willingness to be vulnerable with each other. We have to speak our personal truth to one another on a daily basis. I have to choose to support Dave when we disagree. Dave has to choose to support me whether it's convenient or not.

And we have to quit trying to covertly or overtly change each other. When we said "I do," we didn't say "re-do." Marriage is not a reform school. It is a cooperative, loving relationship between two very different people who serve the same God.

WHO'S IN CHARGE HERE?

After observing other Christian marriages and facing our own frustrations head-on, we chose to get back to the Scriptures. As a result we quickly determined that Jesus had become an *addition* to our relationship rather being in the *center* of it where He belonged.

No matter what we've been led to believe, there is not a human being alive who really controls himself. Whatever is lord of our lives controls us. The woman who lives in hopes of being accepted by her husband is controlled by that husband. The man or woman who lives to "do it my way" ends up controlled by the god of this world, the destroyer, who has always promised that "ye shall be as gods."

In our study, we came across some words that we must have forgotten somewhere along the way: "Fear the Lord your God, serve him only" (Deuteronomy 6:13).

Why is the Lord to be Lord of our lives? The answer is clear when we consider the options. The Lord is the only One who can control us without destroying us. In fact, it is only when Jesus is the Lord of our lives that we truly find ourselves.

In both the "unhealthy hierarchy" and the "isolate" stages, one partner has replaced Christ's authority with another's authority. If you cling dependently to your spouse, you are making him or her your caretaker. When you allow an imperfect human being to be your god, he (or she) will inevitably fail you and you will resent him.

If you cling to independence, either as a controller or as an isolated partner, you make yourself your own god and will seek people to be "need fillers" for you. After a while you realize their inadequacies and imperfections and abandon them emotionally and/or physically.

James H. Olthuis writes:

Sin distorted the relation between man and woman . . . no longer a helpmate, woman would become a competitor rather than a companion. Man would take advantage of the woman's natural yearning for him in order to rule over her . . .

Thus, what has been called the battle of the sexes is actually the abnormal result of the Fall. Man-in-sin will attempt to dominate woman as if she were just a part of the creation to be put under his feet; yet man himself is also cursed and the entire creation with him . . .

It is important to emphasize that the curses of the Lord are just that—curses, not commands to be obeyed. They are the Lord's infallible description of mankind's future in sin . . . the words of the curse are not norms to guide our male/female relations.[1]

Whether married or single, no matter what kind of relationships we're involved in, we are to live by the words of the new commandment, not by the curse. "Love one another. As I have loved you, so you must love on another" (John 13:34).

Loveless Power	Powerful Love	Powerless Love
Focus on me	Focus on us	Focus on you
Emphasis on getting	Emphasis on giving to self and others	Emphasis on giving and giving up
Dominates	Resolves	Yields
Demands	Discusses	Denies
Negates others	Builds self and others	Negates self
Reacts	Responds	Retreats
Uses others	Frees others	Is used by others
Self-motivated	Christ-enabled and internally motivated	Externally motivated
Usurped	Chosen	Forced

FOUNDATIONS FOR RESTRUCTURING

Interdependence, or partnership, is a choice that only a person who has responsibly "individuated" can make. By individuated, we mean having become responsible for oneself as an individual. Partnership is only possible when both parties have chosen to take personal responsibility for themselves and their growth. This process rarely happens to both parties at the same time.

When either partner takes a step towards interdependence, the delicate balance in the relationship shifts. Change, even positive change, brings anxiety. It almost guarantees that the persons you are dealing with will try their hardest to push you back into your old way of life. Every relationship seems to have an equilibrium. When one person initiates a change, the other often struggles to maintain the status quo. It's a bit like a delicately balanced mobile. The whole thing wobbles crazily if just one small part of it is touched.

Nevertheless, restructuring is vital if an interdependent partnership is to be achieved. And a good, solid foundation has to be laid.

Foundation Stone #1. I own my need for a personal relationship with Jesus Christ, who provides me with both power and love.

Our adequacy is not in ourselves but in God. Because of the power of Christ's Spirit in his life, Paul could say, "I can do everything through him who gives me strength" (Philippians 4:13).

The Holy Spirit has chosen to work through us. Each of us is called by God Himself to be Christ's feet, arms, hands, legs, smile, ears, and eyes to those special people we relate to. We are intended to be God's love connection, but that is only possible if God is making His character traits a reality in our individual lives.

Spiritual and emotional growth is the natural consequence of communion with God: "But the fruit of the Spirit is
love, joy, peace, patience, kindness, goodness, faithfulness,
gentleness and self-control" (Galatians 5:22).

Whereas the world attempts to change the way things
look and the way things feel, God changes our inner being. Ezra
Taft Benson once said, "The Lord works from the inside out.
The world works from the outside in. The world would take
people out of the slums. Christ takes the slums out of people,
and then they take themselves out of the slums. The world
would mold men by changing their environment. Christ
changes men, who then change their environment. The world
would shape human behavior, but Christ can change human
nature."

**Foundation Stone #2. I adopt Christ's integration of
love and power in relationships.**

We are fascinated with the pecking order of things. Christ
never was. In Mark 10:35–45 there occurs an interesting inter-
change between Jesus and the sons of Zebedee. James and
John boldly ask Jesus if they can sit on either side of Him in
glory. Jesus informs them that they don't know what they are
asking.

It doesn't take long for word of this conversation to filter
back to the other disciples. They are furious. They probably let
James and John have it in no uncertain terms. Jesus gets wind
of the conflict, and these are His words in verses 42–45: "You
know that those who are regarded as rulers of the Gentiles lord
it over them, and their high officials exercise authority over
them. Not so with you. Instead, whoever wants to become great
among you first must be slave of all. For even the Son of Man
did not come to be served, but to serve, and to give his life as a
ransom for many."

In Philippians 2:5–8 the apostle Paul explains that although Christ was equal with God, He emptied Himself of heavenly glory and took on the form of a slave. Picture for a moment

the Creator of the universe washing the dirty feet of His disciples or allowing Himself to be hung on a cross.

Powerful love, in Richard Foster's words, "comes from above and is not filled with bravado and bombast. It lacks the symbols of human authority; indeed its symbols are a manger and a cross. It is power that is not recognized as power. It is a self-chosen position of meekness that to human eyes looks powerless. It is the power of the 'wounded healer.'"[2]

Foster once told us the story of a dying man who was so ill and so depressed he could only lie on his stomach and face the floor. His dignified, well-known pastor went to visit him on his deathbed. Without thinking twice, the pastor got down on his hands and knees and gently encouraged the man, looking up into his face. The old man never responded, but his son could not forget the humility of the pastor. Today the son— Richard Foster himself—is the beloved author of *The Celebration of Discipline* and several other best-selling books.

How do we imitate Christ? In order to be Christ-like, we first of all acknowledge that we are all equal before God. There are no "little" people—men or women—in Christ's kingdom. God, through Christ's death on the cross, established the equal value of both male and female. In Galatians 3:28 we read, "There is neither Jew nor Greek, slave nor free, male nor female, for you are all one in Christ Jesus."

Christ's death on the cross settled once and for all the issue of our identity. Each of us was declared highly significant, deeply fallen, and greatly loved. The cross leveled both men and women before their Savior. Each must make an individual response to Christ's offer of salvation. "The true way to be humble," Philip Brooks once said, "is not to stoop until you're smaller than yourself, but to stand at your real height against the higher nature of the Lord Jesus Christ. That shows you what the real smallness of your greatness is."

There is no one-upmanship at the cross. Scripturally we must accept the full personhood of both male and female. The Bible does not denigrate either men or women, just sin in both.

Second, if we find ourselves in a position of leadership, be it in a work setting or in a marriage, we must lay aside our concept of headship as synonymous with power. Of course there is a God-given authority structure in all of life. But no matter where we find ourselves along the ladder, we relinquish our "right" to control and manipulate other human beings and we take on the form of a servant in all our relationships.

If you are to be married, or are contemplating marriage, this principle is extremely relevant and sometimes misunderstood. Both husband and wife in a Christ-centered marriage are called to mutual love and mutual submission. They are each exhorted to serve the other. To the husband Paul writes, "The husband is the head of the wife as Christ is the head of the church, his body, of which he is the Savior" (Ephesians 5:23).

We must shed the idea that headship is synonymous with power. That definition comes from our culture. In many companies, if I am the boss, I get to call the shots. By contrast, the headship Paul is talking about means that the husband is leader within a relationship of equals. His headship is not exercised so he can glory in feelings of superiority. It is exercised for his partner's benefit.

Willingly, husbands are to affirm their spouses in their respective journeys toward wholeness and completeness rather than feeling threatened by them. Headship does not mean one-upmanship. In reality it is one-downmanship. Christ, the Head, is our prime example of a servant. Christian husbands must follow His example and become servants, not bosses. They must have deep, unselfish, self-sacrificing love for their wives, just as Christ has for the church.

C. S. Lewis has some sobering thoughts on headship in his classic book *The Four Loves.*

The husband is the head of the wife just insofar as he is to her what Christ is to the church. He is to love her as Christ loved the Church—read on—AND GAVE HIS LIFE FOR HER. (Eph V, 25). This headship, then, is most fully embodied not in the husband we should all wish to be but in him whose marriage is most like a crucifixion; whose wife receives most and gives least, is most unworthy of him, is—in her own mere nature—least lovable. For the Church has no beauty but what the Bridegroom gives her; he does not find, but makes her, lovely. The chrism of this terrible coronation is to be seen not in the joys of any man's marriage but in its sorrows, in the sickness and sufferings of a good wife or the faults of a bad one, in his unwearying (never paraded) care or his inexhaustible forgiveness; forgiveness, not acquiescence. As Christ sees in the flawed, proud, fanatical or lukewarm Church on earth that Bride who will one day be without spot or wrinkle, and labours to produce the latter, so the husband whose headship is Christ-like (and he is allowed no other sort) never despairs. He is a King Cophetua who after twenty years still hopes that the beggar-girl will one day learn to speak the truth and wash behind her ears.[4]

The need for servanthood is crystal clear. It is impossible to share our faith in Jesus Christ by word or by example with someone we are treating as a doormat, or with someone we have placed on a pedestal, or with someone we are exploiting, manipulating, or using to meet our needs.

Something in all of us fights being a servant, and it's often at this point that we find ourselves procrastinating in the initiation of love. Herein is discipleship fought out—our will versus God's. Are we committed to God's way or aren't we? We hope your answer is "I will be a servant in my marriage regardless of my spouse's response or lack of it." Husbands need God's power flowing through them. Without it, it is an absolute impossibility to be to your wife what Christ was to the church.

Just as I imitate Christ's integration of love and power in relationships, I also become aware of what God hates. Hatred is an "against" emotion. In a sense, we are what we love. God differentiates Himself from evil by saying that He "hates" certain things. Proverbs 6:16–19 tells us that He hates

- haughtiness
- a lying tongue
- innocent blood shed (which amounts to abuse)

- wicked plans
- a false witness (dishonesty)
- strife spread among brothers (gossip and troublemaking)

God doesn't relate to people in these ways, and He hates it when others do. And as Christ's disciple, I am to follow His example in my relationships.

And what about submission? There seems to be as much confusion tied to this word as there is to the concept of headship. Scriptural submission is a positive, voluntary result of putting Christ first and being filled by the Holy Spirit. Elaine Stedman defines it this way:

> Authentic submission is not reluctant nor grudging, nor is it the result of imposed authority. It is rather a chosen, deliberate, voluntary, love-initiated response to another's need. It is an act of worship to God, whom we serve in serving others. In no way, then, is authentic submission a violation of our humanity. It is appropriate to the purpose for which we were created, since in serving His creatures, we are serving and worshipping our Creator. And it acknowledges the dignity of our humanity because it is service freely rendered from a will surrendered to the loving purposes of God.[4]

Foundation Stone #3. I own my personal need to be in relationship.

Wounds from our past often result in our making a strong commitment to hide from others. We anticipate this equation: relationship = pain. We can even hide spiritually: "All I need is God." We pull away, saying "never again" and retreating into a safe shell. Imagine this journal entry.

Child, what are you doing behind this high, thick wall?
I'm crying, Lord.

Where did the wall come from?
I built it, Lord, from disappointments. I worked hard. For mortar, I used my tears, mingled with fears and doubts.

But I've given you so many lovely gifts of wisdom and hope and encouragement. What have you done with them?

Oh, I've taken good care of them, Lord. They're over there, hidden out of sight. Someone will rob me if I keep them with me, you see, so I've buried them. In fact that's why I built the wall in the first place—to protect what little I have.

But child, those good gifts were to be used as building materials for your house of wisdom. They're part of your inheritance from Me—no one can take that from you.

I didn't have enough to build a house, Lord.

If you had put your disappointments with your other gifts, if you'd used them to strengthen the foundation of your house, you would have had enough. And I would have gladly given you anything else you needed.

I didn't know I was supposed to keep my disappointments with my blessings.

All things come from Me, child. I turn everything to gold in the end, anyway.

I was far too busy building my wall to build a house of wisdom, Lord.

Wouldn't you have been safer and happier living in a golden house, sharing your treasures with your friends, than crouched out here in the shadow of this ugly wall, crying your eyes out?

I was afraid. And I didn't think I had enough to work with.

Haven't I told you a thousand times not to fear? And you've always had enough. Surely you realize that by now.

OK. I'm sorry. I guess the wall is a mistake. But what about my house of wisdom? Is it too late to build it now?

First tear down your wall, child. Gather your disappointments from the rubble and bring them to Me along with all your other treasures. Let Me help you. It's never too late.

First John was written, at least in part, to counteract our self-protective ways of thinking and behaving. Spirituality is horizontal as well as vertical—it reaches out to people as well as up to God. God not only resides in heaven, in His Word, and in His omnipresent existence, He also resides in those who love Him. First John 4:12 says, "No man has ever seen God; but if we love one another, God lives in us and his love is made complete in us." Our Christian faith is one of incarnational theology.

We desperately need each other, even if our need means that we might get hurt. Faced with the betrayal of Judas and the horror of the cross, Jesus offered His deep and final words to humankind: "A new commandment I give you: Love one another. As I have loved you, so you must love one another. By this all men will know that you are my disciples, if you love one another" (John 13:34–35).

As we are loved by Jesus Christ and as His love is fleshed out in us, even in our broken places, so we are to love others, as Christ did. Christ loves us with a never-ending, serving, personal, noncondemning, responsible, and unconditional love. As we experience that kind of love it is supposed to flow out of us and wash over those around us.

The "body of Christ" image, as described in 1 Corinthians 12, is familiar to most Christians, although we sometimes seem to apply it to church service rather than daily living. Our need for each other can also be depicted by the way the redwoods in northern California support their own ecosystem. How do they survive? They grow in groves, their roots intricately intertwined. No matter how violent the storms that the Pacific Ocean hurls against them, they continue to stand. To uproot one is to uproot them all.

That is the way we can continue to stand in our personal storms. If our roots are intertwined with the roots of others, we can hold each other up.

Whether we are married or single, employees or employers, mother or fathers, sons or daughters, or friends, we need each other. And no matter what the relationship, the idea of submission to one another, following Christ's example, is both costly and rewarding.

WHAT WE MUST LOSE IN ORDER TO BE INTERDEPENDENT

LOVELESS POWER PERSON	POWERLESS LOVE PERSON
Must give up his/her entitlement—"I do nothing menial."	Must give up his/her entitlement—"I don't have to make decisions, think, and so on."
Must give up the last word in decision-making.	Must give up freedom not to make decisions but to criticize those who do.
Must stop using people.	Must stop idolizing people, making them gods.
Must give up his/her narrow perspective of "how it should be."	Must give up his/her lack of perspective of "how it should be."
Must stop game-playing.	Must stop game-playing.

WHAT WE GAIN IN INTERDEPENDENCE

I am receiving and experiencing Jesus' love and power.

I am honoring my Maker by becoming the individual He intended for me to be and by fulfilling His vision for my life.

I am more aware of myself, including the issues I bring into my relationship from my past.

I am more open and accepting of other people and their perspective.

I am in touch with my feelings.

I refuse to carry responsibility that isn't mine.

I am free to grow.

I am growing in my self-honesty and self-respect.

I am experiencing a healthy sense of autonomy.

I can forgive myself.

I can ask for help when I need it.

I can be me and still be in relationship.

I can encourage another's growth.

I can forgive.

I give to another out of choice, not obligation. How they receive my giving is their choice.

I am a safe person to relate to.

I am able to be intimate.

I am open to all life has to offer.

Notes

1. James H. Olthuis, *I Pledge You My Troth: A Christian View of Marriage, Family, Friendship* (New York: Harper & Row, 1975), 9–10.
2. Richard Foster, *Money, Sex and Power: The Challenge of the Disciplined Life* (New York: Harper & Row, 1985), 204.
3. C. S. Lewis, *The Four Loves* (New York: Harcourt Brace, 1971).
4. Elaine Stedman, *A Woman's Worth* (Waco: Tex.: Word, 1976), 33.

4

POWER'S BATTLEFIELD: CONFLICT

Gail rolled over, groaned, and wearily pulled the pillow more firmly over her head. For the third time in less than an hour, the angry argument in the apartment upstairs had awakened her with a start. This time the bitter, profane dialogue was being punctuated with the crash of dishes.

"You—!" shrieked a shrill, female voice.

The man's answer was nothing more than a monotone, but it was noisily accompanied by the impact of another shattered plate.

On and on the debate raged, continuing without respite for nearly half an hour. Suddenly Gail sat bolt upright at the sound of a loud thump. Something heavy had hit the floor above her head. The caustic remarks stopped momentarily—long enough for Gail to wonder if either Judy or Ron had been knocked unconscious.

I wish just once they'd fight during the day, she thought to herself, staring grimly at the numbers on the glow-in-the-dark digital clock dial: 1:30 A.M.

Judy and Ron had been married just six months. They were both in their early forties, and it was a third marriage for each of them. Gail didn't know them well, but she had chatted with Judy one afternoon about their frequent fights.

The two women were alone in the laundry room. Judy was a pretty blonde woman with an athletic, trim body. "I hope we don't disturb you with our knock-down-drag-outs," she laughed. "We're both learning to deal with our anger."

You call that dealing with your anger? Gail thought, smiling in spite of herself. She tried do be tactful. "Well, I'm not going to pretend I don't hear you. But what do you mean, you're dealing with your anger?"

"You see, we're in a recovery group, and we're learning that we both have a lot of anger inside from our dysfunctional families. We aren't really angry at each other, but we're venting our anger by expressing it."

You're not really angry at each other? I hope I'm not around if you ever get angry! Gail shrugged and chuckled, "I guess all I need to know is when to call the police! If I hear bodies hitting the floor, should I dial 911?"

Judy giggled, lifting her laundry basket in her arms and heading for the door. "Oh, don't worry! We throw things, but we try not to hurt each other. We're really quite harmless."

So now they were at it again, and despite Judy's lighthearted comments, Gail was a little worried. She was also annoyed because their marital spat was keeping her awake. At first she thought how absurd it all was. They weren't discussing issues. They were screaming and throwing things in a wild display of emotional extravagance. For Gail, a quiet, reserved divorcée, it seemed impossible to even imagine participating in an exchange of airborne plates and X-rated expletives.

Then Gail's mind wandered back across the years. She and Barry had never fought. They had never even discussed their differences. Their marriage had been cool, calm, and collected; their divorce, much the same. Neither of them had ever raised a voice, let alone a hand, in disagreement. They had ended their five-year marriage "not with a bang, but with a whimper." At the end they simply smiled icily at each other, settled their finances, and parted.

Gail tossed and turned, her thoughts interrupted by Judy and Ron's seemingly endless diatribe.

Maybe I shouldn't be so critical, she thought glumly. *Maybe if we'd thrown a few plates, we'd still be together.*

Angry, fiery debates. Bitter, icy silences. Troublesome issues. Misunderstandings. Cutting words, too hurtful to forget. These are the earmarks of many interpersonal conflicts. And although controversy is possible, even profitable, without being compromised by any of these painful by-products, they embody our worst fears about conflict.

For some of us, conflict is highly uncomfortable. We avoid it at all costs, pretending that the issues at stake really don't matter. Others of us don't feel normal unless some kind of controversy is swirling around us. Because our childhoods were marked with strife, conflict has become a familiar companion, and we feel a little bored without it.

Whether we enjoy conflict or not, life is full of arguments, altercations, and adjustments. The big question is, How do we handle them? Do we come through them valuing ourselves and the other people involved? Are we motivated by love, or controlled by a need for power?

Conflict is simply a difference in point of view. It occurs in all areas of life, but the home front is probably its most frequent battleground. If you have a great marriage, the two of you will not —cannot—always agree. If you have an unhealthy relationship, you may have found a way to be in total agreement at all times.

The more diverse our backgrounds, the more conflict will arise between us. For this reason, the early years of marriage, while we are learning to adjust to a new spouse, are extraordinarily challenging. Half of all divorces happen in the first seven years of marriage. And, notably, one of the biggest issues to be settled in the initial stages of marriage is how couples choose to handle conflict.

Even the most loving marital rapport will not protect us from life's most severe challenges: tragedy, illness, boredom, anger, disappointment, temptation, and mistakes. Conflict simply means that it's time to return to the drawing board, always with the implicit understanding that marriage is a mutual, permanent, and exclusive union.

Many conflicts in intimate relationships are unconscious ways of adjusting the distance between partners. We fight when we want closeness. We fight when we want distance. If we're afraid that our partner will be unresponsive to a deep need, sometimes we'll pick a fight about something minor and superficial, because it is less threatening.

Some battles are worth fighting and some are not. As we live together, we begin to see what the real issues are in our lives, and whether we want to continue to experience contention over them. Conflict provides us with the opportunity to learn necessary lessons. We shouldn't be too eager to escape the friction—there is much to be gained. Besides, it is fantasy to imagine that two people will grow at the same rate and in the same direction, or that they will face all issues from same perspective. That would be tremendously unlikely, as well as boring.

Whether in our homes, workplaces, schools, or churches, we ought to embrace conflict enthusiastically. For one thing, we are commanded to give thanks in all things, and in every conflict, God has something to teach us. Furthermore, if there is only one side to an issue, then only half of the truth is known. Conflict is worthwhile. It is necessary. Conflict amounts to "iron sharpening iron," if we use it wisely, approach it in mutual respect, and know our goals and move toward them.

THE GOALS OF CONFLICT

- Conflict leads to greater open-mindedness. One of conflict's primary goals is to enable us to discover a more complete sense of the truth.
- Conflict helps us change our patterns of communication. We learn from each situation how to adapt and how to adjust methods that aren't effective in resolving issues.
- Conflict opens up blocked lines of communication. When properly conducted, conflict is carried out with the understanding that whatever is wrong is temporary. After all,

you have faith in God, you respect yourself, you respect the other person. Together you are in search of the best possible solution to the problem confronting you. One of you is not out to change the other.

* Conflict acknowledges that there is a problem requiring communication. It is an exciting opportunity to resolve something, to make things better, to improve daily life.

GIVE YOURSELF PERMISSION TO CHANGE

We are odd creatures. When we try a recipe that doesn't work, we conclude that it's a loser, throw it out, and never use it again. Yet when we are ineffective in our communication patterns, we continue to repeat them over and over again. And not only do we repeat them, but we act them out at an accelerating pitch. Our desperation drives us.

What are our options during a time of conflict? We can choose to

* yield
* withdraw
* win
* struggle to resolve

When we entered marriage, Dave's pattern was to yield and Jan's was to win. This should not be too surprising given the home backgrounds each of us had experienced.

Dave had a severely handicapped sister. She was unable to talk, walk, feed herself, or use her hands in any way. Raised voices had a very negative effect on her, and caused her to cry. You can imagine the effect that had on any honest expressions of frustration Dave might have had. It simply wasn't allowed. The unspoken message in the house? "Good Christian families don't raise their voices. In fact, they don't have conflict at all."

Jan grew up in a home where a good discussion or argument was viewed as a way of improving the mind. Her family enjoyed examining various perspectives, although each member held rather tightly to his or her own opinions. As a result, Jan grew up verbal and opinionated.

You can imagine what happened in our home. Dave consistently retreated and yielded, whereas Jan became very proficient at going for the jugular. If she lambasted Dave with words, he would immediately yield. The issue would remain undealt with. And neither of us was required to be honest.

A MATTER OF "RIGHT" AND "WRONG"

The story goes that three blind men encountered an elephant as they walked down the road. The first blind man walked into the elephant's side and said, "The road ends here. We have come to a wall."

The second blind man bumped into one of the elephant's legs. He wrapped his arms around it and said, "No, it's not the end of the road—it's only a tree."

The third blind man felt the elephant's tail brush against his face. He reached up, grabbed it and said. "It's not the end of the road, or a tree either. It's nothing but a rope!"

We can be like those blind men. Even when our eyes appear to be wide open, we cling to a little piece of the truth, ignoring how that piece fits in with the ideas of others. We fight for the right to be right. Most of us believe that there are really only two choices in conflict: my way and the wrong way. And we proceed to stage a personal battle in order to discredit our adversary. We don't address the issues at all. Instead we attack the credibility of the individual.

If I am a person who uses loveless power, I let everyone else know just how terrible they all are for not accepting my agenda. I try to annihilate the opposition. Then, after my destructive outburst, I feel guilty. I try to be a nice guy for a week. But this behavior only lasts so long, and then the cycle starts again. The problem with the loveless power position is that a lifetime of reacting hasn't prepared us to take action.

Meanwhile, the person who takes the powerless love position uses an altogether different set of tactics. She (or he) says nothing that could be thought of as offensive. Needs are expressed only indirectly, and the word *no* is rarely uttered. Dependents acquiesce to limits set by others by agreeing begrudgingly or by dragging their feet. Outwardly they are compliant and placating, but inwardly they feel helpless, trapped, and victimized. Powerless lovers, faced with conflict, feel suffocated by any new demands placed upon them. They blame others for overlooking them. People have to guess their feelings and wants, and usually guess incorrectly.

It doesn't take too many power struggles for the powerless love person to adopt all the strategies of the loveless power individual. Whenever we are afraid to express our requests directly (perhaps because we are afraid of the other person's response or lack of it), our pain builds. When the pain grows to volcanic proportions, we rage. Unfortunately, because we're still avoiding the threatening subject, we often explode over something that isn't the real issue. Yet, whether or not we realize it, in midst of any conflict, we have an opportunity to make choices. We are not obligated to go onto automatic pilot. If we make certain choices, certain results are guaranteed.

The authors of *When Anger Hurts* describe the process: "When you're loud, others get loud. When you blame, others go on the attack. When you psychologically punch someone, that person punches back. People resist you. What is achieved through anger must be defended that way as well. The intimidated, frightened people you push around will find other ways of defeating and getting back at you. You are never sure if even those close to you are cooperating out of love or fear."[1]

WHY NOT SEE IT MY WAY?

Suppose Dave and Jan go backpacking—each of them climbing different mountains. They climb to the top of their respective peaks and scan the valley lying below. They are both intrigued by a cabin in the valley, so they lift their binoculars to their eyes and study it.

Dave, from his mountaintop, sees broken-down corral fences, rusted out cars on blocks, and piles of dirt and rubbish. He hardly notices the cabin itself.

Jan, from her peak, sees a beautiful, tidy little cabin with a white picket fence, a manicured lawn, and a pond with ducks.

Later they complete their backpacking expeditions and meet at the only cafe in town. As they share their adventures, one of them mentions the cabin. The proprietor, who is refilling their coffee cups, comments, "There's only one cabin like that in these parts."

Dave shakes his head, "That's too bad. It's the most run-down, poorly cared for place I've ever seen. You'd think the owner would fix it up."

Jan looks at Dave in disbelief. "I think the altitude has affected your mind, dear." She remarks. "I've never seen a more immaculate cabin. It's just charming."

What are Dave and Jan's choices?

If they yield, they have to deny their perspective—powerless lovers do this.

If they choose to withdraw from the debate, at least one of them will probably be acting from a controlling position. He (or she) will have to change the subject, or pull out a newspaper or a romance novel and shut the other person out. If either is acting out the role of a loveless power controller, she (or he) will storm out of the cafe, escape in the car, and leave the other with the bill.

If Jan and Dave both feel that one of them must win, they will use any means to force the other person to agree with their perspective. After all, it is the "right" position.

If they choose to resolve the issue, they will listen to each other's perspective, respect the other person's intelligence, and try to reach an understanding. Perhaps Jan will walk with Dave back to the top of his mountain and see the cabin from his point of view. He might do the same with her. Or they might ask the cafe proprietor what he knows about the cabin.

So often we are unable or unwilling to realize that our position may be only partially accurate—we can't see the entire picture. It is incumbent upon each of us to find enough humility to recognize our limitations of perspective, while valuing the perceptions of others. Fundamentally we need to believe that we both can be right and that there is almost always an option we haven't yet considered. When this is our posture, we stand with others as equals, together facing the problem. We are not against people, under people, or over them. Differences are valuable—they are the fertilizer for growth.

Whether we travel in academic circles, are involved in a family, are single or married, work on a church staff, or are employed in some business, the choices remain the same:

YIELD	RESOLVE
YOUR WAY	OUR WAY
WITHDRAW	WIN
NO WAY	MY WAY

Let's take a closer look at our choices.

WE CAN CHOOSE TO YIELD

Powerless love is a weak position, based on personal insecurities. It chooses peace at any cost. It does not have standards, demands, expectations, or vision. It is quick to please and appease, and to seek acceptance. Powerless lovers do not have the courage of their convictions. In negotiation, they capitulate. In leadership, they are permissive and indulgent. In marriage, they yield—at times even before their partner is aware of a disagreement.

We often did this early in our marriage, rather than daring to muddy the waters. Jan didn't realize Dave had differing opinions because he held them inside. It doesn't take very long until yielders honestly believe that they don't count—only their mates do. In many ways, yielders live beneath their mates, all the while telling themselves it doesn't really matter.

Yielders deny past hurts and pretend that all is forgotten. They repress past resentments, feelings, and thoughts and respond according to whatever the other person expects. This is not forgiveness, it is fantasy. In reality, yielders are extremely angry people, but they play the "good-Christians-don't-get-angry" tape in their minds. They are sticks of dynamite waiting to explode.

Unfortunately, buried feelings don't die or disappear. They simply go underground and come forth in another form, such as psychosomatic illness, rage, crying and depression, overreaction, cynicism, or even complete abandonment of the spouse.

Tom and Jane sat facing us in the counseling office. His smoldering hostility was obvious—anger flashed in his blue eyes, and his expression was tense. Jane, a pretty, vivacious brunette looked puzzled and distraught. She glanced at her husband from time to time, trying to read his sullen face. What had gone wrong with their thirty-year marriage?

As we talked to the couple, we learned that in their courtship Tom had been attracted to Jane's wonderfully outgoing personality. She was a take-charge kind of woman, and he needed a wife like that—even his mother had said so.

Jane had been equally attracted to Tom's quiet nature. He appeared to be the "strong, silent" type, so enigmatic and intriguing in films and fiction. But Tom was, in fact, unusually sensitive and unable to express his emotions. He was terrified of risks and wanted to be rescued and cared for. Tom's motto was "peace at any cost," and in order to protect his "catered to" position, he had always yielded in every potential conflict.

In response to Tom's passive behavior, Jane had gritted her teeth, becoming more and more responsible for their lives.

In essence, she became Tom's new mother. Although she hadn't liked to admit it openly, she was disappointed in Tom and resentful of him. The mysterious, fascinating man she married had nothing to offer.

As time went by she had taken on an air of superiority. She'd developed a habit of interrupting his sentences, pointing her finger at him and talking in loud, sarcastic tones. Jane said, more than once, "Nothing would ever get done around our house if I didn't take care of it. If I don't prod Tom, he does nothing!"

Of course their roles had made them both uncomfortable for years. But Jane never imagined that Tom would ever want to leave her. "He couldn't live without me," she'd told herself many times. But Jane was wrong. By the time they reached our office, Tom had had it. He wanted out of the marriage. He had been giving in and yielding for thirty years. He felt emasculated and dead inside. He didn't want to live that way any more.

Our emotional TNT often goes off in mid-life. You've heard the classic lines: "You've had your way all these years. Now it's my turn. I'm going to do my own thing." Off he or she drives in a bright-red Porshe, leaving the spouse dumbfounded. After all, they never argued.

However, yielding isn't always wrong. There is an effective way to do it. We yield when the relationship is more important to us than the issue. We yield if the other person is more competent. Sometimes we wish to affirm him (or her) and the perspective he holds. We also may yield when the time and effort it takes to resolve some small matter would violate other values. There are definite times to yield. Maybe you discover after communicating that you are wrong. Then yield, and do so humbly. Love means *often* having to say you're sorry.

YOU CAN CHOOSE TO WITHDRAW

Remember, the opposite of love is not hate; it is indifference. If you are married to someone who withdraws, you know what indifference feels like. The withdrawer removes himself or herself not only from the conflict, but from the relationship as well. This individual turns away from the person and from the issue. "I live in spite of you, and I live without you."

How manipulative this method is! The person who walks away from conflict disconnects emotionally from hurt while hurting the other with indifference. Distance is stretched between the two and any hope of resolution is dashed.

Of course, there is an effective way to withdraw. You can call a "time-out." But beware—time-outs should not be used to hurt or punish another person. They must always be agreed upon, providing time to get yourselves back together again. Perhaps one person needs to cool down; people with quick, hot tempers would be wise to withdraw until the adrenaline stops surging. Perhaps the other person involved needs to form his or her thoughts—to sit quietly, take a walk, or write in a journal. The parties in conflict should agree to come back and discuss the issue at a mutually acceptable time.

Here's a possible "Time-Out Contract" we thought might be useful to you.[2] You could certainly adapt it to your own relationships or circumstances.

> When I realize that my (or my partner's) anger is rising, I will give a "T" signal for a time-out and leave at once. I will not hit or kick anything and I will not slam the door.
>
> I will return no later than one hour. I will take a walk to use up the anger energy and will not drink or use drugs while I am away. I will try not to focus on resentments.
>
> When I return, I will start the conversation with "I know that I was partly wrong and partly right." I will then admit to a technical mistake I made.
>
> If my partner gives a "T" signal and leaves, I will return the sign and let my partner go without a hassle, no matter what is going on. I will not drink or use drugs while my partner is away and will avoid focusing on resentments. When my partner returns, I will start the conversation with "I know that I was partly wrong and partly right."

> Name _____   Date _____
>
> Name _____   Date _____

WE CAN CHOOSE TO WIN

In marriage, yielders are often matched to persons who feel compelled to win. These diehards believe that their opinion counts but that the yielder and his or her opinions are thoroughly expendable. Would-be winners live against and over their partners. They will often do or say anything it takes to win. They deliver hurt and are highly destructive in their use of anger. They try to apply more pressure, more eloquence, and more logic to strengthen their position, because, of course, there are only two positions—their position and the wrong position.

You can imagine the results if two "win" personalities get together. They are both determined, opinionated, stubborn, narrow-minded, and ego-invested. They are highly insecure, lacking in inner direction. And when there is conflict, they both lose because they believe in either/or. Both find their only reward in revenge. These individuals will do anything, including losing themselves, in order to see the other person lose. Enormous amounts of negative energy are expended in protecting backsides, employing criticism, politicking, masterminding, and second-guessing.

Why must we win?

The teenage years are full of double messages, particularly in Christian homes. Teens are taught that good values include cooperation, kindness, and sharing. In sports, they are constantly reminded about the virtues of team play.

The realities of life, however, are somewhat different. The outstanding player gets the award, not the team player. The diligent student still gets a C because someone else got an A—the curve wasn't in his favor. The social world teaches the teenager that he will be accepted or rejected on the basis of conformity to certain standards and attitudes.

As adults, in business we stress competition and still try to get cooperation. The two don't mix well. The fact is, no matter where conflict occurs, winning is not a viable objective.

There will either be a double win or a double loss. Winning results in damaged feelings, attitudes, and trust.

In her book *Beyond the Power Struggle* Susan Campbell says that four common ideas fuel power struggles:

> 1. *We fear that the past will repeat itself.* Suppose someone you deeply love dies. From that point on you continue to have relationships, but after a short amount of time you forsake them. You don't want to be "abandoned" or left behind ever again. So you sabotage every new friendship that comes along.
>
> 2. *We fear that the future won't work out.* By doing nothing we avoid the anxiety that tells us we're going to make a mistake. This is often seen among the unemployed, where a person who has been fired from one job is afraid to look for another.
>
> 3. *We fear not having things our way.* This may occur because we have never been able to depend on people to meet our needs. We might have experienced a highly restricted environment. Or, we may be extremely narrow-minded and narcissistic. It's interesting to note that most of our attachments to a particular point of view are based on fear: fear that we won't be respected; fear that we won't get what we want; fear that others are against us in some way.
>
> 4. *We fear that we've been betrayed by life.* We may have been hurt and disappointed with circumstances, and in response we take out our anger on others. The natural response to our hostility is that people either avoid us or try to change us. Power struggles are inevitable.[3]

Karen and Jake were in the process of getting a divorce. Because of her anger toward him, Karen decided to prevent Jake from having any contact with their only child, Sean. In order to create as big a breach as possible between father and son, Karen informed Sean, as well as all their relatives and friends, about Jake's faults. "He's no good," she said again and again. "He's a hopeless loser." In her anger, she even made up a story which strongly implied that Jake had sexually molested Sean.

Of course the little boy was confused, and felt deeply torn between his parents. When the custody case eventually was settled, the court gave joint custody to both parents.

Now Jake began to "respond" to Karen's tactics. He never picked Jake up on time. He never brought him back on time. He went out of his way not to cooperate with Karen's work schedule, and sometimes left the boy sitting outside Karen's house "to teach your mother a lesson."

Both parents resorted to sending angry messages back and forth, using Sean as their messenger. Jake stopped paying child support after six months. Karen is presently arranging to have him thrown in jail as a "deadbeat dad."

Who suffers most in this kind of power play? The child, of course. But the parents battle on, each one trying to outdo the other in resentment and revenge. Each wants to *win*.

WE CAN CHOOSE TO RESOLVE

Resolution involves working together, communicating together, achieving goals together. These are accomplishments that neither individual could realize alone. When we seek to resolve issues, we are fully aware that our own position is only partially accurate. We are equally aware that the other person's position is valid, too. Resolution involves self-awareness, imagination, and mutual learning.

We don't seek "your way" or "my way" but the best way. Agreement and solutions must be mutually beneficial. One person's success is not achieved at the expense of the other's. When we respect differing points of view and view them as a way of enriching our own, we have achieved the mind-set necessary to work toward resolution.

Resolution is the goal of partnership and interdependence, whether in marriage, business, friendship, or collaboration. And, needless to say, it doesn't happen overnight. Resolvers learn to respect each other. Together they discuss their emotions. Their hurt, frustration, or anger is constructive because it is honestly communicated. People who seek resolution affirm each other, and together they direct their anger toward whatever it is that is dividing them.

WHAT WE SOMETIMES SAY

Regardless of the conflict, whether it be over finances, procedures, church doctrine, in-laws, or outlaws, the statement most often spoken by the yielder is "I must have seen it wrong. You're right, of course."

The withdrawer says, "What problem? There's no problem. And if you've got a problem, I don't want to discuss it."

The would-be winner is overheard saying, "You idiot! How could you be so stupid?"

The resolver states, "I value you. I'm hurt that something is coming between us. We seem to be in disagreement, but I sure want to understand your perspective. And I'd like for you to listen to mine."

We can choose to view other people's differences either as a source of conflict or a source of knowledge. Expanding our perspective to include other viewpoints doesn't mean we abandon our principles or opinions.

Harville Hendrix has observed that if we agree in principle that others have a valid point of view, we may fight this fact emotionally. To demonstrate, he played a classical music tape for a married couple he was counseling. It was César Franck's Violin Sonata in A. Dr. Hendrix asked the couple to comment on the music after the second movement.

The husband focused on the violin performance in the first movement. The wife focused on the piano theme. "It felt stormy to me," she commented.

Her husband immediately embarked on an educated and somewhat condescending critique of his wife's taste (or lack of it).

Hendrix asked them if they would be willing to listen to the music again. "This time try to hear it from each other's point of view."

To their amazement, the sonata turned out to be a richer piece of music than either one had initially perceived it. Hendrix observed that both partners felt they had a valid point of view. However, both ultimately agreed that the composition was, in reality, more complex than their limited perspective.[4]

HOW WE CONFRONT CONFLICT

Let's take a look at three styles of conflict resolution.

Loveless power	Powerful love	Powerless love
Gives orders without asking or permitting questions	Asks questions, seeks to hear, suggests alternatives	Takes orders without asking questions
Makes demands, gives directions, is defensive if challenged	Respects freedom and dignity of others, can affirm truth nondefensively	Obeys demands
Requires compliance regardless of consent or agreement	Values willing cooperation; works for open agreement and understanding	Complies regardless of feelings
Pushes and manipulates; one-person rule in over/under relationship	Leads, attracts, persuades in side-by-side relationship	Stays in under position
Says, "You do," "You must," "You ought to," "You'd better . . . "	Says, "Come, let's do," "We might have done," "Can we try?"	Says, "I will," "I should," "I must"
Depends on his/her own external authority to motivate others	Depends on internal integrity to motivate	Depends on others to motivate

Generates friction, resistance, and resentment	Generates acceptance, cooperation, and reconciliation	Tries to keep peace at any cost
Separates and isolates	Unites and helps	Pleases but frustrates

QUESTIONS FOR THE AGRESSOR

Do you identify with the loveless power position on our chart? Through the use of power, you may have gotten into the habit of being aggressive in the face of conflict. Perhaps you've bullied or browbeaten others to bring them into agreement with you. Maybe you've disregarded their rights and feelings and thought only of your own.

Here is a group of questions you may want to ask yourself:

- Do I feel I'm in competition with others?
- Why am I afraid of being vulnerable?
- Why do I view vulnerability as a weakness?
- Why am I afraid of listening to others?
- Do I really believe that others are my equals?
- What tools do I use to ensure that I win?
- Do I believe that God is on my side and not the other person's?
- Can I, in the long run, really love and respect someone I intimidate?
- The benefits of needing to win are . . .
- The disadvantages are . . .
- What would happen to me if I gave up my position of power?

For you, we suggest a little time to contemplate a wise old adage: "Do not make yourself so big; you're really not so small."

QUESTIONS FOR THE YIELDER

Did you find yourself on the powerless-love side of the chart? Perhaps you need to examine why you are so uncomfortable with conflict. Is it possible that you don't know how to deal with an overbearing person? Yielders usually have two things in common—they don't know how to say no, and they want everyone's approval. Let's consider something we call the "'No' Sandwich Technique." When we say "'No' Sandwich," we mean you are placing your "no" between two positive layers of communication. It could literally change your relationships.

Layer #1: Your first statement acknowledges that you heard what the other person wants you to do. Here's a chance to practice some feedback skills (more about that in a later chapter).
Example: "I understand that you want me to drop everything and take the car in to be serviced . . ."

Layer #2: Your "No!" Here you state your refusal and why you will not or cannot comply with his or her wishes.
Example: ". . . but I am facing a deadline to get an important project finished."

Layer #3: This amounts to an affirmation of your mate, or something you are able to do to ease the sting of your refusal.
Example: "I will be finished with my work in two hours. I will be happy to take the car in then if it will help."

Here is the "'No' Sandwich Technique" used in another scenario.

Layer #1: "I understand that you want me to watch a pornographic movie with you . . ."

Layer #2: ". . . but I choose not to fill my mind with entertainment that degrades women, men, and sex. I also believe that what goes into my mind can defile me. It's threatening to my femininity when you choose a counterfeit for the real thing."

Layer #3: "I'd love to spend an intimate evening together. You're more exciting to me than any movie would ever be."

It might be extremely helpful for you to memorize these generic statements if you are very passive:
"I understand that you want me to . . ."
"I am unable to do what you demand. If I did, I would not be true to myself . . ."
"I am willing to seek to find something agreeable to both of us. I value you and our relationship . . ."

If your mate keeps persisting in his or her attempt to control you, use what communication experts call the "Broken Record Technique." You are to repeat your "'No' Sandwich" statements as many times as needed with a firm but calm and quiet voice.

You can refuse to be controlled by intimidation. Practicing the "'No' Sandwich Technique" will move you toward being assertive. You are being clear, direct, and open about your feelings, thoughts, and desires. You are cultivating self-awareness (What do I really think about this and why?). You are being respectful, not only of your partner's rights but also of your own.

QUESTIONS FOR THE PERSON WHO WITHDRAWS

Whether you are a controller or a dependent, you may be dealing with someone who leaves the room whenever the two of you have a disagreement. If so, you are definitely feeling angry and frustrated. You may even be experiencing the emotions of helplessness and abandonment. Here are some questions we suggest you ask your adversary when you both calm down.

- "I'm hurt (or angry, or whatever). Did you mean for me to feel that way?"
- "What can I do to make it easier for you to stay and face this issue with me?"

One of Dave's clients beautifully expressed to her mate her frustration with withdrawal: "The thing I want most is to protect my love for you. I never want to feel paralyzed. I never want to feel dead inside. So, I need to tell you when I'm hurting or angry. That's one of the ways I take care of our relationship."

Confrontation can be a blessing or a curse, depending on the techniques we use, the attitudes we adopt, and the motivations we have in our hearts. As we said to begin with, conflict is an opportunity for growth and learning. If you and your spouse, boss, colleague, child, or parent both see it that way, you have some interesting and profitable conversations ahead.

However, if your power-and-love issues are unresolved, conflict may not be the final word in your vocabulary. You may want to keep reading if you, like most of us, need to give some serious thought to another very familiar issue: anger.

NOTES

1. Matthew McKay, Peter D. Rogers, and Judith McKay, *When Anger Hurts : Quieting the Storm Within* (Oakland, Calif.: New Harbinger, 1989), 183.
2. Text of the contract is taken from McKay et al., 137, and is used by permission.
3. Susan Campbell, *Beyond the Power Struggle: Dealing with Conflict in Love and Work* (San Luis Obispo, Calif.: Impact, 1984), 75–89.
4. See Harville Hendrix, *Getting the Love You Want: A Guide for Couples* (New York: HarperCollins, 1990).

5

OVERPOWERING ANGER

I (Jan) sat transfixed by the vicious scene that was playing out before my eyes. A couple who had been seeing me for several weeks were in my office again. Max was a distinguished-looking executive who wore expensive suits, Gucci ties, and a well-sprayed coiffure. His wife, Penny, was well-dressed too, but her face was lined and weary. She looked older than her husband and seemed almost immobilized when he was present.

I had just confronted Max with some behavior patterns that seemed to be negatively impacting their marriage. I could see that he was becoming agitated, but his sudden reaction was quite unexpected. He exploded like a bombshell. He leaped to his feet, shouting and bellowing at me at the top of his lungs. His vitriolic phrases were peppered with obscenities. The message he was trying to communicate was something along these lines: "What do you think you're doing, trying to change *me?* My wife is the one who needs to change. That's why I'm paying you and bringing her here. Don't find fault with me. Fix *her!*"

As he roared and raged, other therapists from our clinic nervously gathered outside the door. A secretary looked in at me, raising her eyebrows quizzically. Still Max rampaged on.

Finally, after a diatribe of more than five minutes, he charged out of the clinic and peeled rubber as he roared out of the parking lot.

I looked at Penny in disbelief. She was staring at her trembling hands, which were folded in her lap. "Penny?" I said softly.

She looked up, her eyes red and brimming.

"Is that what it's like at home?"

Penny nodded. "Yes," she whispered. "That's what it's like at home."

THE POSITIVE SIDE OF ANGER

Normally, anger is a valuable emotion—one that God gave us to let us know things aren't quite right.

- Anger says "I don't like what is happening!"
- Anger tells you something about yourself and your relationship.
- Anger is a response to pain.
- Anger is a sign that danger is threatening.
- Anger is a largely unconscious choice based on years of conditioning.

John Bradshaw says, "A relationship that has no capacity for anger fails to embrace the wholeness of a true relationship."[1] The feeling of anger within us is like an oil warning light in a car. It is a signal that something is wrong. The warning light alerts us to a problem we might not know about otherwise. It advises us that we should take action or there could be serious repercussions. Continuing to drive a car for miles and disregarding the oil light might well result in blowing up the engine. Anger signals that we are hurting, have unmet needs, have had our boundaries crossed, are out of balance, or feel violated or threatened. If we don't take heed when we first feel anger, there may be trouble ahead.

Besides these emergency concerns, anger also assists us in the necessary separation and individuation we need to make with our families as we develop into adults. It also enables us to respond when we are almost too terrified to assert ourselves on behalf of our needs.

Too often, however, as in the case of Max and Penny, anger is used to destroy and abuse others. Rather than making us strong and safe, chronic anger weakens us and leaves us vulnerable to attack. It blocks our awareness of pain. And at its core is the impulse to assign blame and to take on the role of a victim.

HIDING OUR ANGER FROM OURSELVES

Many of us experienced emotional abandonment when we displayed our anger as children. Our parents' actions were swift and sure, and as far as we could tell, when we got mad, their love was removed. In our subconscious, anger and abandonment became intertwined. To protect our most precious relationships, we stopped expressing anger. As a result, our anger was pushed underground where it continued to seethe, building up into a volcanic rage. We may not have lost our temper very often, but when we did, everyone knew about it.

Anger is an easily displaced emotion. We take the anger that belongs in one place and we direct it toward a less threatening target. The classic story about anger begins with the boss who has a disagreement with his wife before he leaves for work. He arrives at the office and is grouchy and critical of his partner; his partner takes his frustration out on a subordinate; this subordinate goes home and yells at his wife who is short with the children who kick the cat. Who knows what the cat does with his irritation? All this gives new meaning to the phrase "chain of command."

John Bradshaw writes:

> One of my deepest personal regrets is that I raged at my children and at my wife in the early days of our family life. I didn't fly into a

rage every day or every week or even every month. But I would store up a gunny sack full of hurts, and when I couldn't take it any more, I would scream, holler and pound on the table. Basically, I would try to scare everyone into doing what I wanted them to do. This was clearly sick behavior, and to some extent I knew it. But when a fit of fury came on, I couldn't stop myself.[2]

WINNING THE BATTLE, LOSING THE WAR

The person ventilating his anger is often experiencing an incredible sense of helplessness. He knows something is wrong, but he tries to make his pain your responsibility. When you refuse to respond, or don't even know what is expected of you, he reacts aggressively: *you* must change. If you choose not to, the angry person will attempt to force the issue with intolerant, fear-motivated force. This angry person may win the battle temporarily, but he is definitely losing the war.

People resist, withdraw, and erect defenses to shield themselves from hurt and to keep from being controlled. At a basic, subconscious level we know that losing the capacity to say no, or to have a choice, is a type of death. We feel suffocated by the loveless-power person. To many people, especially those married to controllers, the relationship does signify death. A part of them dies, and they find it impossible to keep their love for the other person alive. Angry people find few opportunities to receive warmth and nurturing.

> Anger stuns. It frightens. It makes people feel bad about themselves. And of course it warns them to stop doing whatever is offending you. But people gradually become injured and resistant. As soon as they see you, they put on their emotional armor in preparation for the next upset. The more anger you express, the less effective your anger becomes, the less you are listened to, and the more cut off you begin to feel from genuine closeness.[3]

BEWARE OF THE ANGRY PERSON

Isolation and loneliness are ever-present realities in an angry person's life. He (or she) often justifies his reactions by becoming cynical about others. Then, when support is available, he doesn't see it or he minimizes it. Expressed anger wounds both the one who is attacked and the person who is angry. Anger is an ineffective long-term strategy for changing anything or anyone. In short, it doesn't work—as research points out:

- "People who vent their rage get angrier, not less angry" (Travis, 1982).
- "Couples who yell at each other feel more angry afterward, not less" (Straus, 1974).
- "The ventilation of anger stimulates both parties to mounting aggression" (Tauris, 1984).
- "Make no friendship with a man given to anger, nor go with a wrathful man, lest you learn his ways and entangle yourself in a snare" (Proverbs 22:24–25 RSV).

Once anger escalates and verbal or physical abuse enters relationships, it is there to stay. To make matters worse, one confrontation usually starts at the level of abuse where the last one left off. Anger can be a smoke screen that keeps us from facing the pain beneath the surface, allowing the unresolved pain to continue to build. Anger can camouflage many different types of pain. Here are a few:

- Guilt
- Hurt
- Shame (I'm worthless)
- Loss
- Helplessness
- Anxiety
- Fear
- Emptiness
- Abandonment
- Rejection

- Frustrated desire
- Isolation

Our thesis is this:

Anger is not what needs to "come out."
Learn, instead, to express the pain
found at the root of your anger.

Healthy anger expresses our pain to the appropriate person in the appropriate setting, and we'll talk more about that in the following pages. But destructive or displaced anger is power out of control. It operates like a vehicle with immense horsepower—it's traveling top speed, driven by someone who discovers too late that he has no brakes. The Scriptures warn us about angry, loveless power.

- "Some people like to make cutting remarks, but the words of the wise soothe and heal" (Proverbs 12:18 TLB).
- "A wise man controls his temper. He knows that anger causes mistakes" (Proverbs 14:29 TLB).
- "It is better to be slow-tempered than famous; it is better to have self-control than to control an army" (Proverbs 16:32 TLB).
- "A man of great wrath will suffer punishment; for if you deliver him you will have to do it again" (Proverbs 19:19 NKJV).

WAYS OF HANDLING ANGER

Here are some ways you may find yourself responding when you're angry.

LOVELESS POWER	POWERFUL LOVE	POWERLESS LOVE
Destructive Anger	Constructive Anger	Destructive Anger
Reactor	Responder	Reactor
Explode		Implode
Violence		Depression
Intimidation		Burial of anger
Verbal Abuse		Swallowing of anger
Sarcasm		Sarcasm
Fault-finding		Fault-finding
Manipulation		Manipulation
Attack the person not the problem	Attack the problem; appreciate the person	Avoid the problem
Blame others	Take personal responsibility	Blame self
Externalize responsibility	Own responsibility	Internalize responsibility
Aggressive: Revenge	Assertive: Relate directly and honestly	Passive: Retreat

One basic belief will revolutionize my thinking if I am inclined towards either the use of loveless power or powerless love in my relationships. It will also reduce my level of anger dramatically.

I Need to Take Personal Responsibility for Meeting My Own Needs.

Victims and martyrs give their personal power to someone else. I have to acknowledge that I am the one who creates both my own misery and my own happiness. I need to take responsibility for my own attitude and choices, at the same time refusing to take responsibility for those of others.

- If I am in a destructive relationship, I am the one who chooses to stay.
- If I am in a job I hate, I chose it and choose to continue working there.
- If my teenager is driving me crazy, I am allowing him or her to do so.

What a radical difference this belief makes in attitudes and in my lifestyle. It means that from this point on I can never blame anyone else for my feelings, choices, attitudes, or actions. It means I have fewer excuses for feeling angry.

KEEPING A COOL HEAD UNDER FIRE

Along similar lines, two of the most important questions to ask ourselves in the midst of conflict are these: "How have I contributed to the problem? Am I insisting on having the last word?" Certainly we are not responsible for others' actions or reactions. Our peace of mind doesn't depend on anyone else's behavior—but we do have to answer to God alone for what kind of human beings we have been.

We have no control over how another person treats us. We all have desires, but there is no guarantee that our friends, family, and co-workers will meet them. All we can do is talk honestly about our disappointments If the other person ignores our words, we must take our hurts to the Lord. When there is a war going on inside us, there is a natural tendency to murder one another with our tongues. James 1 warns us to keep our tongues under control so we can keep our bodies under control.

If you feel your temperature rising, take a deep breath, count to ten, and ask yourself these questions:

- Am I angry because someone else failed to live up to my expectations?
- Am I angry at myself?
- Am I afraid, frustrated, or hurt, or is my self-esteem low?
- What is really making me angry?
- Have I talked honestly about my anger with the other person?

Be aware that no matter how wisely you feel you've expressed yourself, the other person may feel attacked and become defensive. This might have nothing to do with you. It could be a reaction to excessive criticism in childhood. It could relate to an earlier loss of love or some terrifying retaliation. Perhaps the anger stems from the residue of a past relationship, from personal immaturity, or because of physical or emotional abuse. Whatever the cause, do not be afraid to search out professional assistance if you are involved in a relationship characterized by extreme and constant anger.

Kent and Jenny had been dating for several months when she talked to me about their relationship. "I've always dreamed of a love affair where my boyfriend and I would sort of give and take, and we'd both work at it," Jenny told me. "But with Kent, it's always his way or no way. If I don't agree with him, he blows his top."

"What kind of things do you fight about, Jenny?"

"Well, to be honest it's always about stuff he wants me to do for him. See, he never does anything for me. I don't like to keep score—I really don't—but it all adds up after a while."

"So when you don't do things for him, what happens?"

"He starts yelling at me, or else he sulks." Jenny paused, averting her eyes. Then she added, almost flippantly, "Oh, sometimes he hits me, but he's only done that a couple of times."

"And so you go ahead and appease him?"

"Well, yeah, if I want to be with him, I've learned that I'd better give in."

After we'd talked some more, Jenny learned that she was blaming Kent for something that really was her problem. She had never had a satisfying relationship with her abusive father. Now, as a young woman, she was so desperate "to be with" Kent that she always gave him his way. Her compliance was encouraging him to continue his abuse and control. It was working for him. Why should he stop?

In her desire to receive male love and attention, Jenny was giving in the hopes of getting. She wasn't expressing her needs, and she was cooperating with Kent's manipulation. Jenny was well on her way to becoming an abused wife. Fortunately, she began to recognize her destructive behavior and found the strength to change it.

As is often the case, Jenny's unhealthy pattern of behavior had actually begun with her father's anger and abuse.

PARENTS WITH A SHORT FUSE

As parents, we probably experience more guilt than anyone else with regard to losing our tempers. Sometimes we allow anger to negatively slant our conversations. At other times we feel more surging annoyance than we'd like. At one time or another, all responsible parents fear the loss of control that could lead to abuse.

It is very helpful for us to keep close tabs on our emotional condition: we ought to know when we are stressed. We should communicate our times of emotional weakness to our children rather than blaming them for our reactions. Here are a few red flags:

- Beware of times when you and your child are overly tired, worried, or not feeling well.
- Beware of times when you are disappointed because your child didn't perform as well as other children, or didn't live up to your expectations.
- Beware of times when you are having to deal with his or her interruptions.

- Beware of times when you need to talk about rules. Have these established well in advance of conflict times.
- Beware of times when your child is acting out in ways that remind you of your ex-spouse.

We react in anger toward our offspring for other reasons, too. We get preconceived ideas in our minds and overreact when things don't turn out quite the way we had hoped. In *When Anger Hurts,* McKay, Rogers, and McKay point out five self-deceptions that trigger anger at children.

1. *Children cannot be aware of our needs and should not be expected to cooperate with us in meeting them.*
But parents think, "I want something, so I ought to have it."

2. *Young children are limited in their ability to empathize. Fairness is an impossibility.*
But parents think, "Children should recognize the rights of others. It's only fair that others' needs should come first."

3. *Children resent being manipulated—it increases their determination to assert their autonomy.*
But parents think, "I can make my children different if I just apply sufficient pressure." (Behavior that is controlled by fear rather than by internal controls must be maintained by fear.)

4. *Children are not rejecting us or abandoning us when they disobey.*
But these parents think, "If you really loved me, you would do what I want." Or, "I will make you feel as bad as I do."[4]

As parents, we would be well advised to learn what to expect from a child at various stages of development. One of the most damaging things we can do is to rob a child of his age-appropriate behavior and force him to be a little adult in order to win us the approval of our peers. For example, a two-year-old is not rebellious when he is learning the word *no.* He is exhibiting age-appropriate behavior.

When discipline is required, use "I" messages. And when negative consequences are required, are there any natural consequences that are the direct result of the infraction? Did little

Georgie forget his lunch for the third time this week? Let him go hungry. Did Suzy get more of her tacos on the floor than into her mouth? Make sure she's the one who vacuums under the table.

A few other tips for parents who find themselves enforcing rules:

- If you've sent a child to his room for a particular period of time, put a timer outside the door.
- Don't tease, continually remind, or rub in the child's inappropriate behavior.
- Always carry out the consequences.
- Listen to what the child is saying. You may have misunderstood something.
- Be as quick to reward for good behavior as you are to punish for bad actions.

KEEPING TRACK OF MYSELF

Whether we're parents or offspring, husbands or wives, employers or employees, controllers or dependents, whether we have a quick temper or a steady fuse, we need to be watchdogs, guarding our behavior. Practicing self-analysis means that I need to check myself to see if I'm acting in accordance with my values in the midst of conflict. Am I doing anything that demonstrates disrespect or dislike?

That doesn't mean that I take total responsibility for a failing relationship. It is important, however, that I take total responsibility for myself—my words, my actions, my attitudes. That means becoming rigorously honest about myself. In subtle or even unconscious ways, we sometimes increase the potential for conflicts to escalate. Here are some words and actions that ought to be avoided—no matter how angry we feel.

"These are fighting words!"

1. *Giving advice.* "Ask your boss for a raise. You know we need more money!"
2. *Generalization.* "You women are all alike . . ."
3. *Criticism.* "That's not a good parking job. You almost hit that car."
4. *Blaming.* "If it weren't for you we'd be on Easy Street right now."
5. *Abrupt limit setting.* "That's it; I've had it!" "Forget it." "Stop this instant!"
6. *Threatening.* "If you don't shut up right now . . ."
7. *Using expletives.*
8. *Complaining.* "My life is empty." "All I do is work." "You never help me with the laundry."
9. *Stonewalling.* "No problem. There's nothing to talk about."
10. *Mind-reading or assuming.* "I know what you're really thinking. . . . I know you better than you know yourself."
11. *"Innocent" observations.* "I notice that the dishes haven't been done for the past two days."
12. *Teasing.* "Those slacks must have shrunk in the wash; you're sure having a hard time with the zipper!"
13. *Humiliating statements.* "You used to look good, but now I'm embarrassed to be seen with you."
14. *Dismissing comments.* "Get out of my life. I'm tired of looking at your ugly face."
15. *Put downs.* "You call that a meal? I've gotten better grub at the rescue mission."
16. *Sarcasm.* "Sure you're going to fix it. Just like last time, when we had to call the plumber after you . . ."
17. *Accusations.* "You went out and ——— again, didn't you?"
18. *Guilt.* "Don't you ever learn?"
19. *Ultimatums.* "This is your last chance. If you don't shape up, I'm leaving."

"I didn't say a thing!"

1. Groaning
2. Sighing
3. Clucking sound
4. Tsk tsk
5. Shaking of head
6. Raised eyebrows
7. Pointing a finger
8. Shaking a fist
9. Flipping the bird (obscenity)
10. Folded arms
11. Waving away
12. Chopping motion (for angry emphasis)

"What tone of voice?"

1. Whining
2. Flatness (communicates emotional distance: "I'm not here . . .")
3. Cold, frosty tone ("I'm here, but you'll never reach me")
4. Throaty, constricted (controlled fury)
5. Loud, harsh (attempting to intimidate)
6. Mocking, contemptuous mirth
7. Mumbling under your breath
8. Snickering
9. Snarling

"I can tell by that look on your face . . ."

1. Looking away, looking at the floor (abandonment)
2. Rolling eyes ("Not that again!")
3. Narrowing eyes (threatening)
4. Eyes wide ("I don't believe this!")
5. Grimacing ("I don't like that")
6. Sneering
7. Frowning
8. Tightening lips
9. Raising one eyebrow
10. Scowling

"What you do speaks louder than what you say!"

1. Shaking head
2. Shrugging shoulders
3. Tapping a foot or a finger
4. Moving or leaning toward (to intimidate)
5. Moving or turning away
6. Hands on hips
7. Quick movements or pacing
8. Kicking or throwing objects
9. Slamming doors
10. Pushing, grabbing; slapping or slugging[5]

BEARING OUR SHARE OF THE RESPONSIBILITY

There are also some clear signs along the way that will let us know when we are not taking responsibility:

Anger	Blaming	Self-pity
Upset	Vengeance	Lack of focus
Envy	Helplessness	Impatience
Lack of joy	Control others	Intimidation
Fatigue	Judgmentalism	Obsessiveness
Addiction	Defeat	Self-righteousness
Depression	Self-condemnation	

Naturally, anger and love can exist in the same relationship. But when anger smolders just under the surface, it tends to diminish the quality of love. In time both resentment and indifference gain a foothold. I need to acknowledge that:

- If I haven't communicated my frustrations to the person I relate to, it won't be long before I am angry.
- If the anger isn't owned and worked through, I will become indifferent toward that person.
- If I become indifferent, I will have no feelings, no warmth, and no concern.

CHOICES IN ANGER SITUATIONS

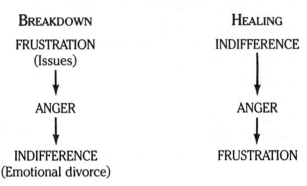

BREAKDOWN	HEALING
FRUSTRATION (Issues)	INDIFFERENCE
↓	↓
ANGER	ANGER
↓	↓
INDIFFERENCE (Emotional divorce)	FRUSTRATION

The opposite of love isn't hate. It's indifference. If I find myself moving toward indifference, I need to take responsibility for my angry feelings. I need to clearly communicate the root of my anger, then deal with the frustrations that started the downward spiral in the first place. It is absolutely crucial to my emotional health that I take responsibility for expressing my feelings, thoughts, and wishes.

Another aspect of taking responsibility is that I need to be honest about the payoffs I receive by abdicating. For example, if I choose to stay in a job with an intolerable boss, I avoid the possible rejection that always accompanies a job search. I also remain financially secure and won't have to learn new tasks.

Or, by staying in a destructive relationship, I never have to face my fear of saying "good-bye," my fear of rejection, my fear of being alone, or my fear of having to survive with no financial assistance. Staying in a toxic relationship instead of divorcing may also enable me to avoid rejection from my church, particularly if it is a conservative one.

When I begin to take responsibility for what I want in life, I have to remember that other people are responsible only for meeting their own needs, too. It is not their responsibility to take care of me and my feelings. (Obviously we are talking about adults, not dependent children.)

First I must meet my own needs, and then I will want to assist others in meeting their needs. At that point I am "loving my neighbor as myself." If I don't take responsibility for meeting my own needs first, I will be giving out of emptiness. I will be giving because I want something in return (like Jenny), such as love, protection, or a change in another's behavior.

But when I give freely, generously, and without an agenda, I am moving toward interdependence. I am moving out of my self-protective ways and into the vulnerability of Christ's way. I am choosing powerful love.

INTERDEPENDENCE GUARANTEES CONFLICT

This all sounds neat and pat. But in reality, when I take personal responsibility for meeting my needs and you take personal responsibility for meeting your needs, our needs are bound to conflict. Disagreements will arise. Competition may raise its ugly head. Discomfort or frustration may manifest themselves.

The more interdependent we are, the more difference our disagreements will make. For example, in an organizational structure, suppose each department supports and disburses its own budget. This arrangement fosters less conflict than one in which all departments must procure resources from a single source. It does not, however, contribute to corporate unity and interaction. In the same sense, a husband and wife with a joint checking account will have more conflict than a couple with individual accounts.

Interdependence may breed conflict, but the conflict is not necessarily bad. It bears repeating: conflict can be the fertile soil of personal growth.

TAKING RESPONSIBILITY FOR OUR ANGER

The Bible says "Be angry and sin not." That is a very short directive that could have been given with a long list of directions. How can we accomplish such a difficult thing? Here are some suggestions that may be of help to you.

1. *Discover the hurt that lies behind your anger.* As we mentioned earlier in the chapter, it is the hurt our anger is masking that needs to come out—not the anger itself. Journaling could be tremendously important to this process. Sometimes we may have to write for a while before we become aware of what really fuels our fury.

2. *Reassure the ones you sometimes hurt.* Let the persons on the receiving end of your anger know that they are important to you. You can communicate your esteem even if you are presently feeling upset.

3. *Ask clearly for what you want.* Be direct, lucid, and nonattacking. Present the facts without judging, blaming, or speculating about others' intentions.

Try to make your requests behavior-specific, regarding only one area at a time. "I think you have been talking about me in front of my co-workers. When you do that I feel embarrassed. I want you to come directly to me if you have a problem with my work. In fact, maybe we could have lunch together tomorrow to talk about specific ways that we could assist each other."

Ask yourself these questions, and then communicate as clearly as you possibly can:

What do I need or want in this situation?
What concerns me about this situation?
What is hurting me in this situation?

And remember:

I am free to want, but others are free to say no.
I have my limits and they have theirs.
I have the right to say no and so do they.
Just because I have a want doesn't obligate someone else to meet it.

4. *Let go, and come to a deep understanding of what letting go really means.* The piece of writing below has helped thousands of people release their loved ones. Think of your own circumstances as you read it.

To let go doesn't mean to stop caring. It means I can't do it for someone else.

To let go is not to cut myself off. It's the realization that I can't control another.

To let go is not to enable, but to allow learning from natural consequences.

To let go is to admit powerlessness, which means the outcome is not in my hands.

To let go is not to try to change or blame another. I can only change myself.

To let go is not to care for, but to care about.

To let go is not to fix, but to be supportive.

To let go is not to be in the middle arranging all the outcomes, but to allow others to effect their own outcomes.

To let go is not to be protective. It is to permit another to face reality.

To let go is not to deny, but to accept.

To let go is not to nag, scold or argue, but to search out my own shortcomings and to correct them.

To let go is not to adjust everything to my desires, but to take each day as it comes and to cherish the moment.

To let go is not to criticize and regulate anyone, but to try to become what I dream I can be.

To let go is to regret the past, but to grow and live for the future.

To let go is to fear less and love more. (Anonymous)

Letting go can take two forms.

- The first is to say, "I'm going to have to live with this just the way it is, so I will release it and my emotions about it to God."

- The second can be more difficult and grim, but at times is expedient. It is simply to say, "This is a toxic relationship. I cannot continue to participate in it. I must let it go altogether." That conclusion can be very painful indeed.

ANGER TOWARD GOD

When our expectations remain unmet, when our dreams don't come true, when our prayers seem unanswered, anger stirs inside us. Eventually we come to realize that life offers no guarantees. Death can visit us. Lost love can occur in our lives. Children can turn away. Whether we are Christians or not, life doesn't magically work out the way we want it to. And when it doesn't, we may begin to rage at God.

Dan and Vicky were married for twenty-five years when the trouble began. Dan had traveled extensively during their marriage and had met a woman on the East Coast whom he'd been seeing for more than seven years. Vicky knew nothing about the affair until she was paying the bills one night and came across some peculiar charges on their Visa® account.

When she questioned Dan, he seemed almost relieved to tell her about Jolene, his lover. This began a terrible struggle that continued until Dan filed for divorce six months later. Naturally Vicky was devastated. Jolene was ten years younger than she and was slim and sophisticated. Dan and Vicky lived in a small town, and before long, everyone had heard about the affair and the impending divorce.

As is often the case, the gossip around town implied that Vicky hadn't been much of a wife anyway. "She's such a stay-at-home," the troublemakers declared. "No wonder Dan was bored. And she is a little overweight, isn't she?"

As if the cruel words of acquaintances weren't painful enough, just as the divorce was about to be finalized, Dan had a sudden heart attack and died.

Vicky, who had been a faithful churchgoer for years, directed all her anger toward God. Why hadn't He taken Dan's life before the shameful divorce? Why had He allowed her to suffer such bitter humiliation? Why had God brought Jolene into Dan's path? Why? She screamed the question at heaven: "Why, God?"

Vicky became more housebound than ever, barely setting foot outside her home. She never darkened the door of her church again. As far as she was concerned, God had betrayed her and she hated Him. She hated the people in her town. And most of all, she hated herself.

We somehow expect God to wave a magic wand that will remove our pain, expel the threat of tragedy, and banish the danger of financial ruin. When He doesn't perform according to our script, we may curse and rail at Him. We may refuse to attend church. Or we may go, but secretly allow our anger to block Him from touching us.

In an excellent article in *Today's Christian Woman* Carole Mayhall makes some wonderful suggestions for us to follow when we find ourselves raging at our Maker. Here, in a nutshell, are her suggestions.

> 1. Write God a letter. Tell Him everything you're thinking, then "give" it to Him.
> 2. Don't let your anger become a barrier between you and God. Listen for His voice and continue to read His Word, no matter how you feel.
> 3. Be careful with whom you share your anger at God. Keep it between you and Him—and if you talk about it at all, make sure it's with a mature Christian who won't be confused by your words.
> 4. Remember—God is with you.[6]

Mayhall concludes her article by saying,

If you ask for bread, He doesn't give you a stone. If circumstances in your life seem unfair, try to look at them from God's perspective. He is a loving Father who wants the best for His children. The difficult times you're going through now may be God's way of preparing you for what He has planned next in your life.

NOTES

1. John Bradshaw, "The Shameful Shock Waves of Rage," *Lears,* June 1990.
2. Ibid., 63.
3. Matthew McKay, Peter D. Rogers, and Judith McKay, *When Anger Hurts : Quieting the Storm Within* (Oakland, Calif.: New Harbinger, 1989), 33.
4. Ibid.
5. The material in this series of lists has been adapted from McKay et al., *When Anger Hurts.*
6. Carole Mayhall, *Today's Christian Woman*, September-October 1992.

6

Powerful Communication

A lady came to a marriage counselor because she had decided she wanted to divorce her husband. The counselor, wanting to save the marriage, asked her a few preliminary questions to see if he couldn't locate and resolve the problem.

First he asked, "Do you have any grounds?"

She answered, "Yes, we have about an acre."

"That's not exactly what I mean. I mean do you have a grudge?"

"No," came the reply, "we have a carport."

Trying a third time, the counselor asked, "Does he beat you up?"

"No, I'm always up before he is."

"Well, then why do you want to divorce your husband?" the frustrated counselor asked.

"Because you can't carry on an intelligent conversation with him!" the wife replied indignantly.

From time to time, we've all found ourselves in conversations like that one. There are people who may speak English, but they certainly don't speak "our" language. To make matters worse, when we do get an idea of just exactly what some individuals are trying to tell us, we are not so sure we want to hear it.

Ralph Waldo Emerson once commented wryly, "What you are shouts so loudly in my ears, I can't hear what you say." We aren't inclined to take people seriously when we don't respect them. And they aren't likely to pay much attention to us if we haven't won their regard. It is quite true, as Scripture says, "Out of the abundance of the heart, the mouth speaketh." Our character lays the foundation for our communication. Who we are significantly determines what we say.

If we want others to listen to us, consider our requests, and respect our wishes, we must be trustworthy men and women—people of integrity. Observers are always assessing our lifestyle. They watch to see if we keep our word. They notice whether we show a deep respect for others.

If we are true to our convictions, we have to be courageous, confident, and willing to confront. At the same time, we will demonstrate a tenderness toward others—for their feelings, their convictions, their welfare. We are to be considerate, empathetic men and women who are willing to listen. Those of us inclined toward loveless power should learn to stop, listen, and respond sensitively. Those of us who operate in the posture of powerless love ought to summon our courage, face our feelings, and express ourselves clearly.

Paul Tournier writes, "Power is the greatest obstacle in the way of dialogue . . . we pay dearly for our power; we live the drama of the lost dialogue."[1]

CHOOSING POWERFUL LOVE

As we begin to move toward powerful love in communication, we demonstrate a commitment toward caring relationships. We are working on many fronts to interact, interface, and interplay with one another.

- Powerful love relies on cooperation instead of bullying.
- Powerful love seeks mutual benefit in all human interactions.
- Powerful love is empowering and nurturing.

- Powerful love is empathetic and has the ability to put one-self in another's place.
- Powerful love takes control only of what is ours to control.
- Powerful love accepts male and female without prejudice or competition.
- Powerful love sees life as cooperative rather than compet-itive.
- Powerful love is based on the belief that there is plenty for everybody; success is not achieved at another's expense.

Just as my character profoundly affects my effectiveness in communication, so concern for relationship sets the tone of what I have to say. If there is no question about my deep feelings in the relationship, then I may blunder and say some things poorly, but they will still be accepted. On the other hand, if I am eloquent and polished and deliver my words flawlessly, but am not speaking as a participant in a loving, caring relationship, my communication will fail.

First Corinthians 13:1 says, "If I speak with the tongues of men and of angels, but have not love, I am become as a re-sounding gong or a clanging cymbal."

ONE CRITICAL PROBLEM

One of the most common problems in interpersonal communication is criticism. It seems to us that the closer we grow toward another person, the more likely we are to criticize. Men and women are equally capable of this vice, and its intensity is always increased by the speaker's history with the person being criticized. Criticism is an attempt to take away another's freedom of choice. We criticize because we are trying to change people from the outside. It is not in keeping with God's way of promoting change, which is always from the inside out.

Criticism can take many forms:

- Unfavorable comparison with others
- Nagging
- Trying to "help"
- Reporting someone else's negative comments
- Finding fault with behavior, physical appearance, or beliefs and values

THE CYCLICAL EFFECT OF CRITICISM

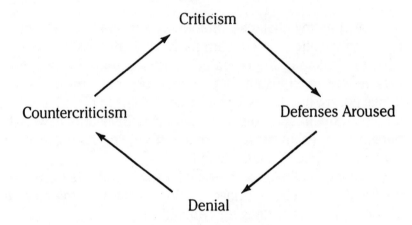

EXAMINING OUR DEFENSES

Defensiveness is a way we protect ourselves from criticism. It puts us on guard duty constantly. Essentially, there are four ways we defend ourselves:

- Denial
- Rationalization
- Blame
- Projection

Although defensiveness is common in all walks of life, please permit us to share a few home-style examples.

WIFE: You're late!
HUSBAND: No, I'm not! (denial)

WIFE: But you promised to be home right after work!

HUSBAND: I got here as soon as I could. I got a phone call just as I was leaving the office. (rationalization)

WIFE: Well, I sure would have appreciated a phone call.

HUSBAND: You're always on the phone with those girlfriends of yours. Why bother? I couldn't have reached you anyway. (blame)

WIFE: Look, I wish you'd just say, "Yes, I was late." You're making this such a big deal.

HUSBAND: You're making the big deal out of it. You're so insecure! (projection)

Logically, the closer we are to someone, the safer we should feel. But the opposite is often true. The closer we grow, the more easily we can provoke anxiety and therefore defensiveness. Often we start out wanting to be close but are always expecting to see indications that the other person wants to move farther away. As often as not, we get what we're looking for.

There are three reasons for our increased anxiety in relationships.

- *Fear of rejection* haunts us. And criticism, even when it is justified, leaves us feeling afraid. "If I'm not perfect, you'll leave me, won't you?" The threat of loss often makes us push away the problem itself. And fear of rejection makes us very defensive.

- *Power struggles* cause us anxiety. Is it going to be my way or your way? This dynamic makes it difficult for us to ask for forgiveness, even when we are wrong. To admit we are wrong feels like a defeat in the power game. So we refuse to acknowledge our faults, at least not without pointing out an equal or worse fault in the other person.

- *Poor self-image* often lies behind much of our defensiveness. A critical family background can make us oversensitive to criticism. The more uncertain and insecure we are, the more defensive we become. Because of our need for self-protection, we try to explain ourselves. This familiar pattern is frequently seen in individuals who have the pro-verbial chip on their shoulder. Their personal insecurity causes them to be poised for a fight, just waiting for a critical word. They are, in every sense of the word, look-ing for trouble.

And what does defensiveness accomplish?

1. We personalize everything and hear criticism where none was intended.
2. We get so caught up in pointing out others' faults that we lose sight of our own.
3. We become sparring partners with those around us rath-er than friends.

So criticism breeds defensiveness, and defensiveness separates us from the people around us. Yet there are certainly faults in others. Aren't we supposed to point them out? The truth is very simple:

I can only change my own behavior.
I am only responsible
for my own actions and reactions.

OVERCOMING OUR DEFENSES

There are several ways of overcoming a pattern of criti-cism and defensiveness. Let's consider them.

1. Be a love connection to the other person.

A friend of ours had a dream one evening. She saw her husband lying on an operating table in a local hospital. She recognized the surgeon—He was none other than Jesus Christ.

Jesus turned and addressed our friend: "You are with Me in this operating room. I am using you to bring healing into the life of your husband."

"Lord, what am I?" asked our friend. "Surely I'm not the scalpel You're using to cut out my husband's malignancies."

"No, that's not your use," replied her Savior. "Look again."

Our friend's eyes scanned the operating theater. Could she be the heart machine, the operating table, the light? Each time she asked, the reply came back, "No, not that." Suddenly she saw something she hadn't seen before.

"Lord, am I the IV?"

"Yes, my child. I'm counting on you to keep the clear, life-building nourishment coming to this man you married."

With that our friend awakened. She was immediately aware that too many times she had chosen to be the scalpel in her husband's life, taking it upon herself to excise his irritating habits and strange idiosyncrasies. Now the Lord was saying that she was supposed to provide emotional nourishment to her husband. How had she gotten into the habit of being the scalpel instead of the IV?

Jesus brought the gospel to us, the good news of unconditional love and acceptance. The gospel took away condemnation, guilt, wrath, and—supposedly—nagging. God, by accepting us, gives us value and love. He has declared believers to be free from condemnation and guilt. We need to minister to others the way He has ministered to us. As His love connection, the IV from God Himself, we have the privilege of doing the same thing for the people in our lives. We act positively toward them. We don't try to change them.

Although this is true in every relationship, it is particularly so in marriage. To share life with another person and to accept each other with ever-deepening understanding is the crowning glory of marriage. It sweeps away the distancing, destroying, degrading, and devaluing that happens when we refuse to accept our marriage partners just the way they are.

Marriage is not only a ministry to our mates, it is also a ministry to God. The way we accept and encourage our mates, the way we respond to our mates, the way we free our mates —all these are ways we minister to the Lord. When we don't accept our mates as gifts from God's hand, we accuse Him of grossly mismanaging our lives.

Love always has open arms. If we close our arms, we are left holding only ourselves. What is the ultimate symbol of open arms? It is Jesus Christ on the cross of Calvary. As His love connection to the world, can we refuse to open our arms, our thinking, and our loving?

2. Give yourself and the other person a break.

Just because you *feel* criticized doesn't necessarily mean you are *being* criticized. Just because your colleague said he didn't agree with a section of your report doesn't mean he's attacking you. Just because your mother hasn't phoned in a few days doesn't mean she's upset with you.

Nothing defeats defensiveness like honest self-appraisal. If you are in a relationship in which you can clearly see the other person's flaws but your own seem too trivial to mention, perhaps your defenses and your pride are clouding reality. Only denial tells us we are perfect. God is the only perfect One. We are all dysfunctional. You're not OK and I'm not OK, but the good news is—that's OK!

Rationalization tells us that we could be perfect if it weren't for outside, uncontrollable circumstances.

Blame tells us that the fault lies elsewhere.

Projection tells us that others are flawed, not us.

In Romans 3:10, Paul says, "There is no one righteous, not even one." To make a long story short, we're all in the same boat.

3. Accept responsibility for your own attitudes and words.

Apart from miraculous answers to prayer, only four elements lead to behavioral change.

- Acceptance
- Openness and vulnerability
- Affirmation
- Pain and negative consequences

When we abandon criticism, manipulation, angry outbursts, and icy disapproval, we are left with these four wonderfully effective ways of bringing God's transforming love into the life of another person. Combined with prayer, they can work miracles.

Learning to Accept Others

As a way of living out God's unconditional love to others, we can choose to bring a new perspective to our relationships. Once we stop condemning and start accepting we come to the realization that two are better than one.

What does acceptance do? It releases other people from the fear of being condemned. It models the love of Christ, it breeds acceptance, releases others to grow, settles confusion, breaks down barriers, and broadens our perspective. True love says, "I love you unconditionally, not only for the privilege of loving you, but for what loving you makes of me."

Differing Views of Acceptance

	Loveless Power	Powerful Love	Powerless Love
Identity Found:	Through myself	Through grasping God's love and acceptance	Through another
View of Self:	I am all that I need	Positive and realistic: "I am highly significant, deeply fallen, greatly loved"	I am nothing

	LOVELESS POWER	POWERFUL LOVE	POWERLESS LOVE
View of Others:	Use them	Value them	Worship them Fear them Cling to them
View of differences:	Seeks uniformity; will expose, criticize	Accepts and compliments	Seeks uniformity and security; is critical of self and partner

WILLING TO BE VULNERABLE

When we are willing to express our hurts and our powerlessness, we render ourselves defenseless. This reinforces the other person's freedom of choice. If I express my pain, but refuse to use personal power to change the situation, I am being honest, but not manipulative. Let's look at a few examples.

- "I am very, very sad when you choose the self-destructive behavior of using cocaine."
- "It hurts me deeply when you call me names."
- "It really made me feel bad when you ignored me at dinner."
- "I felt so sad when I found out you'd disobeyed me like that, especially after you agreed not to do it again."

When power, anger, control, and resistance have failed us, we are left with vulnerability. The result may be empathy on the part of the other person. The New Testament calls this empathy "godly sorrow [that] brings repentance" (2 Corinthians 7:10). Jesus embodies this truth. We've hurt Him, wounded Him, and grieved Him. Instead of calling down powerful forces to crush us, He adopted the ultimate example of vulnerability: He died on the cross for us.

GIVING STROKES AND REWARDS

Affirmation is a wonderful reinforcer. People who love power misuse affirmation. In their hands, affirmation becomes a cheap form of flattery, a tool to get the other person to do whatever they want. Powerless lovers don't always mix affirmation with truth; they, too, use it to flatter for their own ends. But honest, positive reinforcement builds up people as well as relationships.

COMMITTED TO AFFIRMATION

LOVELESS POWER	POWERFUL LOVE	POWERLESS LOVE
I want my own way	I love you and me	I idolize you
You are useful	Both of us are valuable	You're valuable; I'm worthless
For the purpose of manipulation	For the good of the one affirmed	For the purpose of manipulation
Performance based	Person and performance based	Person based

Each of us chooses daily whether to leave "heartprints" or heartaches on the lives of those we encounter. We can train ourselves to be aware of other people's strengths. Robert Schuller writes, "Perfect love perceives people not as problems but as possibilities."

Jesus did this for us. He never labeled us as sinners, but He commanded that we "go, and sin no more" (John 8:11 KJV). He always restores our hope, saying, "You are the light of the world," "You are the salt [seasoning] of the earth," and—even more wonderful—"I have called you friends" (see Matthew 5:13–14; John 15:15).

EMPLOYING NEGATIVE CONSEQUENCES

You've probably heard about "tough love." From time to time all of us have to exercise its principles in our lives. We learn that we have to let people experience the unpleasant results of their behavior in order to inspire change. In the New Testament, the prodigal son's father allowed his son to wallow in the filth of the pigsty. He didn't rescue him or criticize him. He simply let him go. But he waited outside the house for the boy, hoping in his heart that when things got bad enough, his son would come back home.

Addicts, philanderers, and abusers don't change because of nagging and criticism. They change because their faces have hit the pavement one too many times. They change because their enablers have finally thrown them out. They change because they are losing everything they hold dear. And sometimes this involves a direct confrontation. As James Dobson says:

> I certainly believe in the validity of unconditional love, and in fact, the mutual accountability I have recommended is an expression of that love! For example, if a husband is behaving in ways that will harm himself, his children, his marriage, and the family of the "other woman," then confrontation with him becomes an act of love. The easiest response by the innocent partner would be to look the other way and pretend she doesn't notice. But from my perspective, that is tantamount to a parent's refusing to confront a fourteen year old who comes home drunk at 4 A.M. That mother or father has an obligation to create a crisis in response to destructive behavior. I'm trying to say that unconditional love is not synonymous with permissiveness, passivity, and weakness. Sometimes it requires toughness and discipline and accountability.[2]

Cause and effect is a law of the universe. And it can be a contributing factor to change. When the effect grows too unbearable, the cause has to be reconsidered. Once we have done all we can do, the rest is up to God and the free will of the person we care about.

At this point our communication should be with God—an ongoing pouring out of our concerns, requests for His intervention, and thanksgiving that with Him, nothing is impossible.

4. Accept Responsibility for your needs and communicate them.

Many quarrels between individuals reflect hidden questions about relationship and are not about issues at all. Am I important to you? Are you concerned about my wishes? Do you consider me in your decisions? Of course, when we use issues as a smoke screen, we aren't really making our questions clear, nor are we answering them correctly when they are asked of us.

Deborah Tannen says:

> It is something like the practical joke that can be played using a dual-control electric blanket. If you reverse the controls, the first attempt by either person to make an adjustment will set off a cycle of worsening maladjustment. I am cold. I set the controls beside me higher, you get too hot and turn your controls down, so I get colder and so on. The attempts to correct actually increase the error. Once the wiring is in the wrong place, efforts at change are palliative or worse.[3]

Each of us has to check his own wiring. What if you consider it "normal" to talk loudly, and you are in conversation with someone who considers it "normal" to speak softly. You try to encourage the other person to speak up by speaking up yourself. Your friend decides to set a great example for you by lowering his voice even more. As you both try to remedy the situation, you are in fact aggravating it. Each person is unintentionally provoking the other person to increase his offending behavior.

Perhaps we should begin by asking ourselves:

- What do we want from the other person?
- Why do we want it?

After we have clarified these two issues for ourselves, we can begin to work on making our request. This request should include the answers to both questions.

If you are able to express yourself in writing, you may wish to give your thoughts to the other person on paper. Otherwise, you may choose to use written words to help prepare yourself for a conversation. If necessary, ask your friend to write a list of your behaviors that may be causing difficulty. If you both set realistic time goals for the correction of these behaviors, you will quickly see your friendship, marriage, or work situation transformed quickly and effectively.

Time and again counselors discover that the people with communication problems often lack in themselves what they'd like to see changed in the other person. Harville Hendrix writes:

> While it was often true that what one partner needed the most was what the other partner was least able to give, it also happened to be the precise area where that partner needed to grow! For example, if Mary grew up with caretakers who were sparing in their physical affection, she most likely has chosen a husband, George, who is uncomfortable with bodily contact; the unmet need in Mary is invariably matched by George's inability to meet that need. But if George was to overcome his resistance to being affectionate in an effort to satisfy Mary's needs, not only would Mary get the physical reassurance she craved, but George would slowly regain contact with his own sensuality. In other words, in his efforts to heal his partner, he would be recovering an essential part of himself.[4]

5. Speak the truth in love.

In Ephesians 4:15, Paul tells us to "[speak] the truth in love." Constructive honesty builds up. Destructive honesty tears down. Sensitive speakers are necessary—and in rather short supply. One author made this point sarcastically: "The Bible tells us that Samson killed ten thousand Philistines with the jawbone of an ass. I am convinced that an even greater number of conversations are killed daily with the same instrument."

Suppose you're in a staff meeting explaining a key project of yours when a colleague slings a stinging criticism your way. Momentarily you are taken aback, and your mind races for a comeback that will save your credibility. Of course we dislike being put on the defensive, but it happens often in the workplace. The criticism may not be personal, but we often find ourselves reacting as if the critic were out for blood.

What should we do?

1. Take a deep breath. Separate from the incident enough to focus on the big picture. People are more apt to remember your composure (or lack of it!) than your specific response.
2. If the criticism is unfounded, incorporate the critic's objections into your response. "That occurred to me too, but I felt it wouldn't present a problem because ... That's something I need to consider. Thanks for pointing it out."
3. Try to figure out something you might agree on and redirect the conversation to that point.
4. Whatever you do, don't become rude, sarcastic, or personally insulting.

None of us, in any setting, has been given a license for rudeness. Words leave permanent imprints. Martin Buber defines a true dialogue as one in which "the speaker has the other person's individuality and special needs in mind." Loving dialogue is accepting, understanding, and empathetic. The words you use say much about you. The way you express yourself is an outward manifestation of your inner attitude.

Research confirms that in face-to-face conversations, 7 percent of a message depends on the words, 23 percent on the tone of voice, and 70 percent on nonverbal body language. Do you demonstrate love and grace in your choice of words, your tone of voice, and your body language?

Many of us have learned to avoid difficult issues by avoiding each other. At first, Curt and Dianne tried to communicate, but they never really succeeded. Dianne would hold in her emotions until she was ready to explode. Once she was seething, Curt would sense her anger and rush out the door—out of her presence. He was afraid he would lose his temper, hurt her feelings, and damage their relationship. By the time he came back, Dianne had decided the confrontation wasn't worth the trouble, and so she acted like nothing had happened.

Although they were well-educated people, both Curt and Dianne found it extremely difficult to express their emotions in words. They loved each other very much, and the thought of loss or abandonment paralyzed them. Meanwhile, their fears were building a wall between them, aggravated by resentment and frustration.

For years, neither of the two was willing to take the emotional risks necessary to bring issues into the open and talk about them. And as time went by, the thicker the barricade became and the less they talked about anything. Their daily conversations became mine fields. They had to tiptoe through the simplest dialogue to avoid hitting explosive issues.

No one ever blew up. No one ever spoke up. Curt and Dianne lived in fear of destroying their relationship. And ironically, the relationship was nearly at an end when they finally came for help. Relationships cannot survive if problems aren't aired and resolved.

Love and friendship do not include mental telepathy. Don't expect another person to know that you are upset, needy, or confused. Tell him. Express yourself. There is nothing so bad that it cannot be made even worse by brooding silence.

COMMUNICATION STYLES

LOVELESS POWER	POWERFUL LOVE	POWERLESS LOVE
Communicates to get you to understand me	Communicates to understand us better	Communicates to understand you better
Truth talk	Balance of truth and grace	Grace talk
Uncomfortable with vulnerability (fears rejection)	Risks vulnerability (affirms acceptance)	Refuses to be vulnerable (fears rejection)

LOVELESS POWER	POWERFUL LOVE	POWERLESS LOVE
Inflicts pain with words (destructive honesty)	Expresses hurt and relieves pain (constructive honesty)	Repeats pain (dishonesty)
Uses you and I statements	Uses I statement	Uses you and I statements
Silence of anger and withdrawal	Silence of empathy and understanding	Silence of fear and avoidance

6. Accept responsibility for becoming an active listener.

Paul Tillich has written that the first duty of love is to listen. The way we listen has a much greater impact on people's self-esteem than the way we talk (unless our talk is abusive).

Concentrated listening tells the other person that he or she is important to us, as are his ideas, feelings, and problems. Listening conveys respect and dignity, and it is a powerful means of modeling God's love. "I waited patiently for the Lord; and he inclined unto me, and heard my cry" (Psalm 40:1 KJV).

To be a great listener, you have got to make some choices. You will have to say yes to differences. You must also be willing to drop your preconceived notions about the speaker. To listen well is to care about the other person's feelings as much as you do your own. It is to acknowledge that there are no boring people, only disinterested listeners.

Carl Rogers points out that the "the major barrier to mutual interpersonal communication is our very natural tendency to judge, to evaluate, to approve or disapprove the statement of the other person."[5] When you draw a person out by asking interesting and probing questions, then react with negativity, judgment, and condemnation, you will shut the door to future communication.

People need to talk when they are going through hard times. When someone is having difficulties, your providing a shoulder to cry on will be more important than giving "sage" advice. Here are a few classic conversation stoppers:

1. "It will turn out OK. Things have a way of working themselves out." Reality: Some things don't. Failure and tragedy are real. To the person hearing this platitude, it feels as though you are minimizing his problems.

2. "It isn't that bad." To the other person, it is.

3. "Think positively. You have a lot to be thankful for." Thanks for the gift of guilt! Your judgment that the other person has no right to feel discouraged or inadequate isn't right.

4. "Things could be worse." That's exactly what he's afraid of. Your friend wants to remedy the situation before it gets worse.

5. "Cheer up. Let's talk about something else." That informs the listener that his or her feelings are intolerable to you, or that you're bored with his concerns.

6. "What you're really feeling is (fear, anger, hurt, and so on)." The communicator will retreat quickly if he or she feels analyzed rather than heard.

7. "You shouldn't feel that way." This implies that the listener is the judge of what is right and that feelings must always be logical, rational, and controlled.

8. "The Lord must be trying to tell you something." This amounts to a guilt trip—or worse, a bad case of you trying to read God's mind.

9. "Let me share this verse with you . . ." This is another way of saying "I can't tolerate your feelings, and I'm about to lay the whole matter to rest by nailing you with Scripture."

10. "God doesn't give us any more than we can handle." When anyone is in a crisis, it feels overwhelming. Telling the person that God will never give us more than we can handle is a way of minimizing another person's pain.

11. "You're tough. You can handle it." The listener is longing for comfort and encouragement. Telling the person he can "handle it" is another way of saying, "It's your problem, not mine. Don't bother me."

12. "It wouldn't have happened if you hadn't . . ." Finding fault adds guilt to the person's already-painful problem.

THE VALUE OF FEEDBACK

When real understanding is desired, feedback is essential. We know you believe you understand what you think we said, but we're not sure you realized that what you heard is not what we meant! Confused? That's the reason we need feedback. But what is feedback?

- Feedback is repeating, in your own words, what you heard the other person saying.
- Feedback is also communicating the feelings you perceived beneath the words.
- Feedback includes no judgments, evaluations, or opinions. It simply reflects back to the other person what you think you heard.

Unfortunately, the more important the message you're trying to get across, the greater the danger of misunderstanding. Are you thinking about having a landmark conversation with someone? Here are a few tips for discussing major issues with important people in your life. You'll soon see how important feedback can be to the outcome.

Plan your dialogue. Careful thought, timing, and feedback are vitally important. Make sure you have chosen a good time to talk. If need be, get away from others and find an opportunity to converse alone.

Think before you speak. As clearly and simply as possible, describe the cause of your concern. Always use "I" statements to avoid projecting blame or criticism at the other person. If you find it difficult to define the emotion you're feeling, try checking this list. I am feeling

hurt	inferior	tense
humiliated	silly	loved
lonely	jealous	rejected
intimidated	sympathetic	disappointed
hatred	accepted	frustrated
hated	protective	impatient
confident	angry	superior
shy	sad	ashamed
useless	cheated	trapped
jubilant	unworthy	despairing

Ask for a response. Speak for a short time (we recommend thirty seconds), then ask the other person to paraphrase as accurately as possible what he or she heard you say.

Ask how he (or she) thought you were feeling as you said it. Ask how your words and feelings made him (or her) feel.

Respond to the feedback. Either acknowledge that the person indeed got your message, or clarify it. After you have restated it, ask him to repeat back what you said.

At first you may feel clumsy using the four steps involved in feedback. But if you will exercise them over a period of time, they will improve your communication skills dramatically. Just remember, it takes practice and time to master these skills. Give yourself and other people grace.

LISTENING

LOVELESS POWER	POWERFUL LOVE	POWERLESS LOVE
Better talker than listener; listens when it serves his/ her purposes	Listens to better understand others, self, and to gain broader perspective	Listens intently to get clues on how to "fit in"

LOVELESS POWER	POWERFUL LOVE	POWERLESS LOVE
Can ignore words and feelings behind words	Listens for feelings as well as words	Listens for feelings behind words
Listens defensively	Listens with feedback and acceptance	Listens defensively
Rejects criticism	Weighs criticism	Internalizes criticism

Good communication can help us overcome our tendencies toward powerless love and loveless power. As we search for the right words to express ourselves, we clarify our issues, crystallize our feelings, and consider our motivations. Communication, along with commitment, are the two powerful pillars that support healthy, valuable relationships.

My Communication Covenant

I will tell you that I value you.

I will tell others that you are special.

I will talk to you politely.

I will initiate compliments and affirmations.

I will affirm your character whether you succeed or fail.

I will accept your perceptions as legitimate ones.

I will enjoy your uniqueness.

I will make time for you.

I will show my appreciation for you in practical ways.

I will laugh with you.

I will listen to you without preoccupation, judgment, or criticism.

I will listen to your feelings as well as your words.

I will be honest with you.

I will reach out when I need you.

I will be open with you.

I will be flexible with you, understanding that life is an
   ever-changing reality.
I will not try to possess you.
I will be gentle with you.
I will continue to work at understanding myself.
I will keep your confidence.
I will be loyal to you.
I will respect you and your perspective.
I will be your friend.

Notes

1. Paul Tournier, *The Violence Within*, trans. Edwin Hudson (San Francisco: Harper & Row, 1978), 128.
2. James C. Dobson, *Love Must Be Tough* (Dallas: Word, 1983), 56.
3. Deborah Tannen, *That's Not What I Meant* (New York: Ballantine, 1986), 121–22.
4. Harville Hendrix, *Getting the Love You Want: A Guide for Couples* (New York: HarperCollins, 1990), 156.
5. Carl Rogers, "Communication: Its Blocking and Facilitation," *ETC: A Review of General Semantics* 9, no. 2 (1952). A publication of the International Society for General Semantics.

7

SEX: POWER OR EMPOWERMENT?

R hoda is a tiny woman, slender and pale, with huge brown eyes. Her hair is disheveled, and her expression is frequently vacant and detached. At about the time Rhoda was admitted to our hospital, I (Dave) noticed a front page story in the newspaper, reporting that a local school principal was being accused of sexual misconduct. I glanced at the story, made a mental note of the man's name, and promptly dismissed the details.

In the meantime, Rhoda, my patient, had become deeply depressed, almost to the point of suicide. In our daily conversations, she was having a difficult time remembering portions of her childhood. Although I suspected some kind of sexual abuse, I waited to see if God would begin to bring things to her memory. Before long, He did.

The horror Rhoda experienced as her flashbacks began nearly destroyed her life. She began to remember being molested by someone at school. An adult male. No, not a teacher. Then the story began to spill out, and it was one of almost unprecedented misconduct.

The school principal—the very one I'd read about in the paper—had sexually abused more than thirty-five little girls over several years' time. Rhoda had been one of them. But she had been even more unfortunate than most of the others.

The perverted man had not been content to fondle and perform indecent acts upon the female students in his principal's office. He had gained permission, because of his respected role in the community, to become the legal guardian of Rhoda and eight or ten others. Over a period of years, he had enjoyed access to these little prisoners whenever he wanted to use them. When they grew too old to tantalize him, he found new victims. And, like Rhoda, every one of girls this school principal abused is permanently damaged.

Man vs. Woman: An Overwhelming Problem

The misuse of sex—loveless power at its worst—demonstrates the drive to control, to put a human being under one's complete domination. More often than not, we see it in male overpowering female, although the opposite also exists. In most cultures, male supremacy is an ingrained attitude, which intensifies the impact of sexual power games.

This is not a new problem. In the Old Testament community, women were often treated as possessions to be used and disposed of at male discretion. According to Josephus, Jewish men prided themselves with the "spiritual truth" (taught in the Talmud, not the Pentateuch) that women were inferior. Yet those same men used women in polygamous relationships and for prostitution, both in and out of the temple.

Into this sinful, arrogant environment came Jesus Christ. God chose to make His only begotten Son dependent on a woman for His birth, care, and nurturing. Jesus grew into a radically different rabbi who affirmed women. In the fourth chapter of John, we find Christ giving the first revelation that He was the Messiah to a woman. She, in turn, became the first "evangelist" of His gospel.

Jesus regularly taught women the Scriptures and, despite prevailing tradition against it, He held a conversation with a woman in public. According to Jewish custom, a woman was not legally permitted to bear witness, but Jesus' words after the resurrection to a woman were "Go and tell my disciples." New Testament Scripture verifies again and again that Jesus sees women as equally significant to men.

Richard Foster says:

> The notion of female inferiority is a false and soul destroying doctrine. And if we reject the inherent inferiority of the woman, we must also reject the inherent subordination of the woman. . . . We need to be reminded that the rule of the male over the female is not a description of pristine sexuality before the fall but of the curse of the fall; "Yet your desire shall be for your husband and he shall rule over you" (Gen. 3:16). Sexism is sexuality's distortion, not its wholeness.[1]

Surely we've grown more enlightened in our modern world. Or have we? Donald Trump, in his best-selling book *The Art of the Deal,* explains that life is a series of competitions that he, Trump, must win. Many admire and emulate this man for his financial successes. However, his view of women leaves little room for philosophical debate. He states, "You know, it really doesn't matter what they [the media] write as long as you've got a young and beautiful piece of ———."

WINNING THAT PERFECT "TROPHY"

Some men seem to need to reassure themselves of their masculinity by winning sexual contests against other men. In the novel *Bonfire of the Vanities* Tom Wolfe describes certain women as "trophy wives." They are chosen according to various attributes the man finds impressive. It could be brains, income, social skills or connections, number of advanced degrees, heritage, athletic skill, career success, finances, or fame. Of course, in reality, the competition centers on somewhat less noble qualities: youth, good looks, and sexual prowess.

Some competitive executives change wives or girlfriends with each promotion. They don't want to be "undermarried" for a new career position. If the man is aging, he may choose younger women as he moves up the ladder. How familiar and sad is the story of the wife of twenty-five years who, after putting her husband through graduate school, faithfully raising their children, and supporting him through his early career struggles, is discarded at mid-life for a young woman who had seduced him—the distinguished, now-affluent professional.

CONTEMPLATING "THE WEAKER SEX"

Some demeaning attitudes are prevalent throughout society. Even among Christians it is believed that helpless, weak, dependent women are supposed to be attached to strong, creative, dominant men. Here are some other notions.

- A woman must show deference to a man.
- A woman has tremendous healing, nurturing, and sexual powers; those are solely what she is meant to provide.
- A woman has nothing of value to offer a man other than her sexuality.
- Women are less intelligent than men.
- If a woman submerges herself in a man, she will feel safe and loved.
- When things go wrong, a woman is to blame.

In light of these beliefs, the woman surrenders her power and the man acquires it simply because he is male. As the relationship progresses, the equation between the two becomes imbalanced, with power on one side and weakness and fear of power on the other. Women who have swallowed these attitudes are too eager, too willing, too compliant, too giving, too soon. Their eagerness to be involved sexually reveals their lack of self-worth and sense of limits.

When a relationship begins this way, the power alignment for the continuing relationship has been set. The power lines are often drawn on the first date—the woman conveys the strong message that she will "go along," won't rock the boat, will do whatever the man likes. After all, he's the one in charge, isn't he?

The pattern continues in the bedroom. The woman keeps silent while the man pressures her to do things she finds abhorrent. She never communicates her own sexual needs or desires to her lover. She also avoids initiating lovemaking because she fears that her partner will think badly of her or ridicule her if she does.

Who she is is defined solely by the mate to whom she relates. She cannot be true to herself—she has sold out to her partner. If anything goes wrong she immediately attributes it to her failings. She is constantly anxious, reactive, self-critical, and vigilant. She attributes power to others and eschews it for herself, assuming it is personally destructive. Her only value, she believes, lies in fostering the growth of others. She fears that using her abilities and powers is dangerous and somehow selfish—a label she greatly fears. She lives in an inflexible place where "women do this" and "men do that."

A Game Everybody Loses

This sexually overpowered woman has violated her own integrity. She is pretending to be someone she is not. And, because of her choice to stay in hiding, she also keeps her boyfriend or mate from being authentic. So long as women continue to play roles instead of being real people, everybody loses.

> For every woman who is tired of acting weak when she knows she is strong,
>> There is a man who is tired of appearing strong when he feels vulnerable.
>
> For every woman who is tired of acting dumb,
>> There is a man who is burdened with the constant expectation of "knowing everything."

For every woman who is tried of being called an "emotional female,"
    There is a man who is denied the right to weep and to be gentle.

For every woman who is called unfeminine when she competes,
    There is a man for whom competition is the only way to prove his masculinity.

For every woman who is tired of being a sex object,
    There is a man who must worry about his potency.

For every woman who feels "tied down" by her children,
    There is a man who is denied the full pleasure of shared parenthood.

For every woman who is denied meaningful employment or equal pay,
    There is a man who must bear full financial responsibility for another human being.

For every woman who was not taught the intricacies of an automobile,
    There is a man who wasn't taught the satisfaction of cooking.

For every woman who takes a step toward her own liberation,
    There is a man who finds the way to freedom has been made a little easier.[2]

WHAT WE SAY, WHAT WE MEAN

Language can be a subtle but deadly weapon used by men to attack or demean women. For example, in a professional setting, women don't want to hear "dear," "honey," "sweetie," or "lady."

A young woman surgeon was on her way to the hospital. She had emergency room duty. She passed the scene of an automobile accident and stopped to assist. While she was caring for the injured person a second car stopped. A man came rushing up and pushed her aside, saying, "Stand back, lady! I know first aid!" The woman was Dr. Jeanne Petrek, the first woman ever to receive a full-time faculty appointment in the Emory University Medical School Department of Surgery.

Young men and some so-called adult men talk about having "scored" the night before. The implication is that women are objects placed on earth for man's use. This kind of thinking is reflected in the dirty jokes repeated in male company.

Professional women, who confront sexual bias and harassment with some frequency, especially appreciate receiving compliments. But if their male co-workers only comment about their appearance and never take note of their quality of work, the "compliment" continues to undermine the woman's self-worth.

To illustrate this kind of thinking, take a look at this tongue-in-check guide for telling a businessman from a businesswoman:

> A businessman is aggressive; a businesswoman is pushy.
> He is careful about details, she is picky . . .
> He's depressed (or hung over), so everyone tiptoes past his office;
> she's moody, so it must be her time of the month.
> He follows through; she doesn't know when to quit.
> He's firm, she's stubborn.
> He makes wise judgments; she reveals her prejudices.
> He is a man of the world; she's been around.
> He isn't afraid to say what he thinks; she's opinionated.
> He exercises authority; she's tyrannical.
> He's discreet; she's secretive.
> He's a stern taskmaster; she's difficult to work for.[3]

Please don't categorize this as "women's lib" material. What we're talking about is valuing each other as equals, regardless of gender or race. Galatians says this about Christians: "There is neither Jew nor Greek, there is neither slave nor free, there is neither male nor female; for you are all one in Jesus Christ" (3:28 RSV).

When we build relationships on an unequal basis, we cheat ourselves of wonderful interaction, deeper understanding, and valuable friendships. But that is not the worst of it.

A LOOK AT DISTORTED SEXUALITY

C. S. Lewis discussed the dangers of indulging in sexual desire apart from Eros, or "being in love."

> Sexual desire, without Eros, wants it, the thing in itself; Eros wants the Beloved.
>
> The thing is a sensory pleasure; that is, an event occurring within one's own body. We use a most unfortunate idiom when we say, of a lustful man prowling the streets, that he "wants a woman." Strictly speaking, a woman is just what he does not want. He wants a pleasure for which a woman happens to be the necessary piece of apparatus. How much he cares about the woman as such may be gauged by his attitudes to her five minutes after fruition (one does not keep the carton once one has smoked the cigarettes). Now Eros makes a man really want, not a woman, but one particular woman.[4]

Pornography is a prevalent form of sex without love. It is only concerned with the physical activity of lust. It is cut off from relationship and from the full range of emotions, intellect, and spirituality. Pornography is a dehumanizing exercise of sexual power that cheapens, deceives, and destroys.

Pornography is a power play designed to affirm women's inferiority, implying that they have no right to set limits in a sexual relationship. In pornographic books, magazines, and films, the woman follows every dictate of the man's depravity. Men are depicted hurting woman in the course of sexual activity, tying them up, hitting them, attacking them violently.

Hard-core pornography involves sadism, the infliction of pain on another human being, and masochism, a perverse stimulation experienced while suffering pain. The goal is pain, not connection. Pain actually masquerades as a substitute for a healthy sexual relationship. It is a counterfeit—dehumanizing and destructive.

Sexual abuse, which is frequently the acting out of pornographic ideas, occurs whenever one person sexually dominates and exploits another. This may involve either overt activity, such as rape, or it can be more indirect, such as when a date pressures a woman to go further with him than she wants to. A better understanding and definition of sexual abuse helps women find the courage to report mistreatment and to protect themselves from further undesirable encounters.

A SEXUAL BILL OF RIGHTS

In *The Sexual Healing Journey: A Guide for Survivors of Sexual Abuse*, author Wendy Maltz includes in her list of sexual rights:

1. The right to develop healthy attitudes about sex.
2. The right to sexual privacy.
3. The right to protection from bodily harassment and harm.
4. The right to say no to sexual behavior.
5. The right to control touch and sexual contact.
6. The right to stop sexual arousal that feels inappropriate or uncomfortable. . . .
8. The right to enjoy healthy sexual pleasure and satisfaction.[5]

Perpetrators of sexual abuse sometimes confuse their victims about these rights. And although offenders may try to convince themselves and their victims otherwise, sexual abuse does not occur by accident. Abusers either intentionally harm or take actions they know could cause harm. Either way, they rob and misuse their victims.

TAKING ADVANTAGE OF SEXUAL VULNERABILITY

Peter Rutter is a psychiatrist who conducted a landmark study, *Sex in the Forbidden Zone: When Men in Power—Therapists, Doctors, Clergy, Teachers, and Others—Betray Women's Trust.*[6] Rutter defines sex in the forbidden zone as sexual behavior between a man and a female patient or client under his care in a professional relationship. It can happen anytime a woman entrusts important aspects of her physical, spiritual, psychological, or material welfare to a man who has power over her. The man could be a male doctor, therapist, clergyman, lawyer, teacher, or workplace mentor.

Women in power can exploit men, too. We knew a woman who offered herself sexually to a pastor. After years of seductively pursuing him, his wall of morality collapsed one night. The next day she became "overcome with guilt" and confessed her sin (and the pastor's sin) to the elders of the church. Naturally the pastor was finished—his reputation was ruined.

It turned out that, as a child, the woman had repeatedly been sexually abused by a teacher. She had an understandable distrust and hatred of men in authority. Her pattern of behavior was to track down men in positions of power, find their weaknesses, and seduce them. Once she succeeded she made their guilt known to influential people. We learned that this woman had left a string of devastated reputations, marriages, and careers in her path. More often than not, however, the male is the sexual headhunter.

Relationships between a woman and her male doctor, therapist, lawyer, mentor, or pastor are ones in which both sexes are invited to invest their strongest hopes, wishes, fantasies, and passions. These are relationships in which the man holds the power and the woman places her trust and hope in him. Day after day men in these positions sit in privacy with women who trust, admire, and rely on them. There is a constant pull toward greater intimacy—toward the misuse of power.

- Businessmen travel with female protégées.
- Women, especially in divorce or custody cases, disclose many of the most intimate details of their marriages to their lawyers.
- Male professors and teachers invite a student's trust.
- Doctors have access to a woman's nudity.
- Therapists and pastors gently provide a comfortable setting where secrets, sexual and otherwise, can be revealed.

The damage a man causes himself is often elusive, because in the moment of forbidden sex he may be able to convince himself that he is satisfying a deeply felt need. Yet by exploiting the woman in order to feel more fully alive, he abandons the search for aliveness within himself. When a man's brief moment of forbidden sexual release is over, he is farther still from access to the life-giving resources within himself.

A man's objective should be to maintain a boundary against sexual contact, not to keep sexual thoughts away. The healing power of restraint is enormous. First of all, the woman is valued entirely apart from her sexuality, and she is safe. Furthermore, the man taps into a vast inner reservoir of hidden strength he previously didn't know he had.

UNWELCOME SEX IN THE WORKPLACE

Sexual harassment amounts to unwelcome sexual advances in the context of employment. These advances can be verbal or physical. In classic sexual harassment cases, the boss is the culprit—a male in a position of seniority. But women most often find themselves harassed by co-workers, who may not have influence over their jobs but do have the power to create an environment that is demeaning and degrading.

Much sexual harassment goes unreported. Why?

- Women fear reprisals on the job.
- They fear loss of privacy and want to keep it a secret.
- They lack conclusive proof.
- They want to end the harassment as painlessly as possible.
- They fear that if they sue the company they will be blacklisted and unable to get another job in their field.

Darlene is an attractive woman in her forties who had a positive, professional relationship with Frank, her boss, for almost four years. But gradually, to her discomfort, he began to say little things that disturbed her. She felt there were subtle innuendos in some of his statements.

Then one day, with a wink he remarked, "I'm going to get a couch for my office. That way both of us can use it." That comment, which made Darlene shake her head in disbelief, began a nightmare of harassment for her.

Before long, the man was pouring out, in detail, his sexual problems with his wife. Darlene tried to find reason to leave the room in the midst of those tasteless conversations, but the minute she returned, there was Frank, persistently coming back to the exact place he'd left off.

"Frank, you need to talk these things over with your wife, not with me," she advised him one day, trying to keep her voice firm and even. The next afternoon, he started in again, this time going into more graphic description than ever.

By now Darlene was readjusting her hours in an effort to avoid Frank. She no longer looked him in the eye when he spoke to her, and she avoided every possible encounter with him in the office.

She was annoyed to receive a notice about a Saturday staff meeting—her weekends were her one escape from the constant pressure of Frank's pursuit. She attempted to excuse herself, but Frank insisted that she had to be there. When Darlene arrived at 10 o'clock sharp, Saturday morning, Frank was the only other person at the office. He tried to intimidate her into having sex with him.

She managed to escape. But the following Monday morning, Frank called her into his office, closed the door, and started pleading with her again. "You don't understand! I've got to have you," he repeated hoarsely.

"Look, Frank. You're married. This has to stop."

Darlene loved her job. She had grown and learned a great deal about financial management there. She didn't want to quit, and she struggled with her thoughts. Who could she talk to? What were her options? Frank was the only boss.

After a few more failed seductions, Frank finally gave up. But soon thereafter, he became highly critical of Darlene's work performance. He began to address her as "Ms. Smith," rather than Darlene. He overloaded her with work and found fault with everything she did.

In less than a month's time, Darlene resigned. As her therapists, we were the first people to hear her story. She had never told a soul.

Darlene's case may have been exceptional, according to Louise Fitzgerald, a psychologist at the University of Illinois. She says that only about 25 percent of sexual harassment cases are about botched seductions. Joyce Brothers writes that sexual harassment is a power issue and is about putting the woman down, humiliating her, and keeping her "in her place." It is a tactic to control women rather than a matter of sexual desire.

We have heard all about sexual harassment, particularly since the media focus on the Clarence Thomas congressional hearings. But what are we to do about it when it happens to us? Here are a few ideas that might help.

1. *Approach the harasser directly.* If you feel overwhelmed at the thought of confronting the person directly you might put your objections in writing. Approaching the harasser directly, in person or in writing, sends the message loud and clear and makes the victim less powerless. Be direct and detailed. Identify the behavior that makes you uncomfortable, explain how it makes you feel, and say what you want to see happen. Keep a copy for yourself.

   You might want to say something like this: "Look, I know you can find any number of women who would be happy to oblige you, and all they would want is a nice evening out, not a job. But I'm interested in the job. I can do competent work for you. Please let's have a business relationship. Give me a chance to show you the professional quality of work I'm able to do."

2. *Follow up your conversation with a typewritten memo.*
   Restate your objections, and keep a copy for yourself. If
   the response you receive is "I was only kidding," don't
   worry. The person knows you aren't kidding. If the harassment continues, you have documentation to show
   that you tried to resolve the problem.

3. *Keep a log of what is happening, including times, dates,
   and places.* Keep track of where incidents occur. Photo-
   copy any letters or graphic material. Talk to other wom-
   en in your office to find out if there is a pattern with the
   offender, and allow them to give their support.

4. *If things don't change, officially report the offender.* Go
   to his supervisor, to personnel, or to the person sug-
   gested by company policy. Keep a copy of all written
   reports.

5. *Decide what your next move should be.* Perhaps you
   are not satisfied with the response of your company,
   or maybe the owner of the company is the person ha-
   rassing you. If you work for a small company, there
   may be no formal policy for dealing with sexual harassment. You are facing a choice. Either you will have
   to leave your place of employment, as Darlene eventually did, or you will have to seek the support and
   advice from your union, a lawyer who has this as a
   specialty, or governmental human rights agencies.

   There is usually a time limit during which you can
   file your complaints. Weigh the risks, the possible
   drain on yourself, and the chance that you may not
   win. If you decide to move forward, be prepared for a
   battle, and don't wait too long.

SEXUAL POWER IN INTIMATE RELATIONSHIPS

Eroticism is big business in the United States, and has
been so since the '60s. Sex is used to sell everything from cars
to furs. We compare ourselves to all sorts of sexual models in
film, television, music, and print media. Americans have a mania
for statistics—sex researchers bombard us with information,
and we often find ourselves not competing well with "national

averages." Why all the focus? For many people, sex is the only affection they ever get. They give sex in order to receive love.

In their book *American Couples: Money, Work, Sex,* Philip Blumstein and Pepper Schwartz say that it is women more than men who keep sexual score.[7] Women measure their femininity by how their husbands respond to them sexually. When a man is unable to demonstrate affection out of bed, sex may be his wife's only means of feeling attractive to him, of getting stroked and experiencing closeness. Women are often devastated when their spouse shows little or no sexual interest in them.

In a book called *What Really Happens in Bed,* University of Illinois psychologists Betsy Tolstedt and Joseph Stokes reported the results of their research on sexuality and romance. In a sample of 1,000 couples, divorce was likeliest to occur not because of disappointing sex, but because emotional and verbal intimacy were missing. Time and time again women told them they felt totally besieged sexually.[8] Of course sex is exciting. But without other forms of love—hand holding, romantic dinners, lingering embraces—eventually sex can become a source of female rage.

In 1986 columnist Ann Landers did a nationwide survey of 90,000 women. Seventy-two percent said that, given the choice, they would rather be held close and treated tenderly than have intercourse. Forty percent of these women were under forty.

With all this in mind, it is not difficult to see how sexuality becomes a power game in intimate relationships. Powerless lovers submit to sex to receive affection or find themselves denied sex because they are being "taught a lesson." Loveless power individuals expect sex on demand, or use it as a weapon. Let's look at a few ways sex and control get mixed up in our private lives.

1. As we've already pointed out, sex becomes the only means of receiving affection.

2. Sexual humor is used destructively—jokes in public, making fun of one's spouse in private. "Thunder thighs" are not funny to the person who is battling the bulge.

3. Clothing becomes a control issue. Either the female is expected to look sexy when she goes out, or she's condemned for trying to look seductive. Either way, the man's fragile ego is the culprit.

4. Sex is limited to when and however one spouse demands it.

5. A spouse is pressured to have sex in ways that make him or her feel uncomfortable.

6. Masturbation is used in anger to pay back the wife or husband for not being stimulating enough, or for not providing enough sex-on-demand.

7. One partner retreats into fantasy—film, pornography, or other exciting sexual media—rather than relating to the real person who shares the bed.

8. Spouses withhold sex from each other.

9. One spouse attempts to seduce the other's friends or family members.

10. One partner has an affair. Perhaps the most powerful tactic of all, this destructive behavior requires certain criteria for its unique type of "romance."

   a. To feel a romantic high with another person, you have to feel somewhat insecure with her or him, not totally sure that he cares.

   b. You have to have not known him well; he must be a little strange and unpredictable.

   c. There must be barriers to your encounter, such as physical distance between you and the need for secrecy.

   d. There must be limits on the time you can spend together.

Superficial though they usually are, affairs are devastating to relationships. Trust is broken, guilt is overwhelming, self-esteem suffers. The husband or wife's positive energies are focused outside the marriage, and problems within the marriage are avoided rather than faced. There is high risk of contracting a sexually transmitted disease, of an enraged spouse's retaliating, or of an unwanted pregnancy developing. And of course the threat of divorce is very real indeed.

11. Sex is used for manipulation. This, unfortunately, has been the tactic of women for generations. One of the most manipulative books on this subject to come off the presses in the last few decades was Marabel Morgan's *The Total Woman*. Everything in it reeks of the kind of sexism that permeates our American culture.

In *Back from Betrayal*, physician Jennifer P. Schneider says of Morgan's book: "The woman who reads *The Total Woman* and incorporates its principles into her life will accept 1) that her husband's love is conditional and that she must buy it by being a perfect housekeeper, a sexy lover and an admirer and servant of her husband; 2) that her own needs and feelings don't count; 3) that her husband needs her in order to feel whole and that she is responsible for how he feels; 4) that her husband has all the power in the relationship; 5) that if her husband leaves her or is unfaithful, it is her fault; 6) that she can control her husband by what she can or cannot do; and 7) that to a man, sex equals love. If she can get him to be sexual with her, then this will prove that he loves her. The Total Woman is thus a Total Codependent."[9]

POWERFUL LOVE: HAPPY, EMPOWERING SEX

We have all witnessed the sad consequences that come as a result of loveless power or powerless love in the arena of sexuality. And, unfortunately, sexuality in the Christian community has also received a tremendous amount of bad press. Christians are often depicted as frigid, sexually repressed lovers who don't really quite approve of what they are doing in the bedroom. Nothing could be—or should be—farther from the truth. Our sexuality was God's idea. It was initiated and created by Him. Our being involved in sexual relationship was planned by God —in fact participation by married couples is commanded by Him.

Throughout the Bible Scripture teaches that sex is a legitimate need, a God-given pleasure. But God's Word clearly emphasizes that our sexual involvement is most lovingly and powerfully acted out in the context of a marriage relationship. Powerful love accepts God's standard not to be involved in premarital or extramarital sex. This standard, by the way, was set for our protection, not to inhibit us. God knows better than anyone else just how destructive these kinds of sex can be.

Powerful love is rooted and grounded in the positive message of the Bible. God wants us to enjoy our sexuality, but love is God's absolute requirement. In fact, God *is* love. The closer we get to this loving God of ours, the greater the possibility of drawing closer to our mates.

God allows His love to flow through us, which empowers us in our marital sexual relationship. Powerful love is characterized by three essential characteristics.

MUTUALITY

Mutuality is the basis for a positive, healthy, growing sexual relationship. The English word *mutuality* comes from a Latin word meaning "exchanged" or "reciprocal." This suggests a back and forth relationship where each person is empowered. You and your spouse are there to promote each other's well-being and nurturing. In order to do this, you will need to do the following:

- both take responsibility for initiating physical intimacy
- both commit to make their spouse their "dream lover"
- both commit to experiment sexually within the context of marriage

AUTONOMY

Autonomy is another basis for a healthy relationship. We need to feel the freedom to be ourselves. I need to be in touch with my body and my needs, and so do you. We cannot have satisfying sex if we are uncomfortable with each other's bodies, either by sight or touch. And our enjoyment will be even more decreased if we refuse to appreciate and accept our own bodies.

If you feel shame and self-consciousness when your partner's eyes see you naked, it may keep you from relaxing into your sexual feelings. Have you ever faced your uncomfortable feelings long enough to ask where they came from?

Three factors determine our body image. They are feedback, sensory input, and the models we hold to. What type of feedback have you gotten from childhood about your body? The amount of touching that you received in your home also affects your body image. Did you learn that you were indeed touchable? What do you envision as an ideal body? We are forever confronted by "beautiful people"—actors, actresses, and fashion models with whom we simply cannot compete. They make us feel fat, frumpy, and forgettable. What a negative impact this has on our sexual intimacy!

If you are willing to be grateful for the body God gave you, and if you are willing to look at its beauty, you will become attractive to yourself and then to your mate.

AUTHENTICITY

It is imperative that we authentically and honestly share our sexual needs with our partner. Couples often do not want to talk during a time of lovemaking. But they fail to set aside another time when they are free to clearly express their sexual needs, desires, and fantasies.

Powerful love pushes for clear direct communication about my sensuality. What turns you off? What turns you on?

More of this? Less of that? We please each other best by being honest about our needs and our responses. We must change our focus from pleasing our partner or performing for our mates to sharing our own pleasure with our mates. It is the most satisfying way to please our spouses.

PHYSICAL INTIMACY

LOVELESS POWER	POWERFUL LOVE	POWERLESS LOVE
I initiate so that I am in control	I initiate and respond to show my love	I refuse to initiate to show who is really in control
I initiate because I have a need	I initiate and respond because this is our need	I respond because it is my duty
I initiate because I want sex	I initiate and respond because we both enjoy sex	I respond because my partner wants sex
I please myself	I please myself and respond to my mate	I perform for my partner

Lovemaking is the culmination of all other types of intimacy that are shared by a man and a woman. As two individuals, we have come to share intellectual unity; we cherish a common understanding and mutual respect with regard to life. Our emotions have become knit together in deep, rich feelings of empathy, spontaneity, and delight. We share a common faith in Jesus Christ and we often agree in prayer together, opening our hearts not only to each other, but to Him.

Now, as man and wife, at last our bodies are joined—both symbolically and in consummation of the intellectual, emotional, and spiritual intimacies we treasure. Beyond the physical pleasure, beyond the romantic excitement, beyond the erotic fulfillment is one incredible reality: we are truly one, and this amazing union is what God intended for us all along.

NOTES

1. Richard J. Foster, *Money, Sex and Power: The Challenge of the Disciplined Life* (San Francisco: Harper & Row, 1985), 106.
2. Nancy R. Smith, *Images: Women in Transition,* comp. Janice Grana, *The Upper Room*, 1976. Used by permission.
3. From Natalie Shainess, M.D., *Sweet Suffering* (New York: Pocket, 1984), 228–29. Used by permission.
4. C. S. Lewis, *The Four Loves* (New York: Harcourt, Brace, Jovanovich, 1960, 1988), 134–35.
5. Wendy Maltz, *The Sexual Healing Journey: A Guide for Survivors of Sexual Abuse* (New York: HarperCollins, 1991), 55.
6. Peter Rutter, *Sex in the Forbidden Zone: When Men in Power—Therapists, Doctors, Clergy, Teachers, and Others—Betray Women's Trust* (Los Angeles, Calif.: Jeremy P. Tarcher, 1989).
7. Philip Blumstein and Pepper Schwartz, *American Couples: Money, Work, Sex* (New York: Morrow, 1983).
8. Steven Carter and Julia Sokol, *What Really Happens in Bed: A Demystification of Sex* (New York: Dell, 1990).
9. Jennifer P. Schneider, M.D., *Back from Betrayal* (New York: Ballantine, 1990), 148.

8

PARDONING POWER

John, a friend of ours, sometimes recounts the story of a first-grade bully who beat him up every day after school. Young John could have set his watch by the assaults—they happened every day at 3:00 P.M., the minute school was out, without fail. The boy was much bigger than John, and any attempt at self-defense only made matters worse. This went on for several months, leaving John's body bruised and his soul battered.

To his immense relief, John's family moved later that year. Before long, they had moved several more times, leaving the bully miles and years behind. But John never forgot his tormentor and the cruel abuse he had suffered at the hands of the bigger boy. He had buried a deep hatred of the bully in his heart, and it never left him.

Not many years ago, John attended a high school reunion. John saw many familiar faces, and one particular face that he'd never expected to see again. To his dismay, John found himself in the company of the the now-adult bully. Unbeknownst to John, they had attended the same high school.

"Do you remember me?" John asked, trying to hide his bitterness. "We were in first grade together."

The man shook his head blankly. "I don't think I've ever seen you before."

In the days that followed, John began to understand that he and he alone had carried the burden of those beatings. The bully had found other victims and had forgotten them as quickly as they moved away or outgrew him.

But from the time he was six years old, John had made room in his heart for the bully. He had carried him and his brutality around like a heavy weight. John had never forgiven, so he had never been set free from the pain.

John's story reminds us of another one—an Asian legend bearing much the same message. Two monks vowed together to abstain from all earthly temptation. They both understood that this meant they would never have contact with females. It was a lifetime vow, and for decades they had kept it.

One day as they walked back to the monastery, it began to rain and the streets were transformed into muddy canals. As the monks approached an intersection, a young girl in her beautiful kimono stood helpless, unable to cross to the other side of the road. One of the monks impulsively picked her up and carried her there.

The other monk was furious. They walked in silence until they came to the gate of the monastery. Finally the angry monk could contain himself no more. He reminded his brother monk of his promise. He pointed out how blatantly he had broken his vow by carrying the young girl across the road, and he demanded an explanation.

The monk who had carried the young woman replied, "I put her down back there on the road. You're the one who seems still to be carrying her!"

No Longer "Due and Payable"

It is true that forgiveness gets the hate and bitterness off our backs and out of our hearts. But forgiveness amounts to far more than the removal of an emotional burden. Forgiveness is a judicial term. Legally, forgiveness means that although I hold a "note" against someone, I choose to tear it up instead of declaring

Relationships are damaged by all but one of these choices

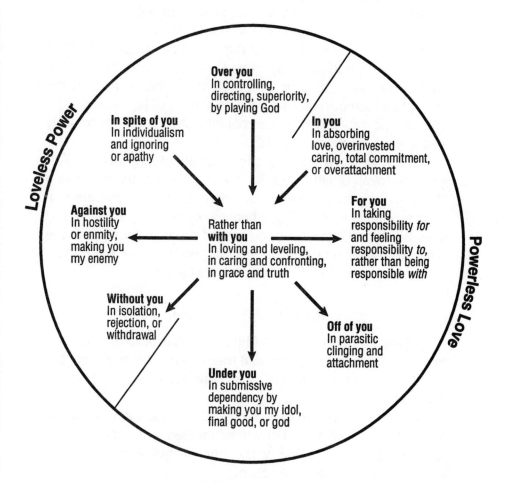

When this happens, forgiveness is required

Adapted from David Augsburger, *Caring Enough to Forgive/Not to Forgive* (Ventura, Calif.: Regal, 1981),19. Used by permission.

it due and payable. That is precisely what we are supposed to do for one another.

People really do owe us. They have sinned against us by dominating us and by living against us, without us, under us, off of us, for us, or in spite of us (see chart, p. 163). Most people have neither the means nor the will to pay us back for their trespasses. That leaves it up to us to remove the debt from our books. The extent to which we are able to forgive them is the extent to which our internal balance sheet will be cleared of all outstanding debts. And a clear balance sheet amounts to a big step toward emotional health.

H. Norman Wright has this to say about forgiveness: "Forgiveness involves letting go. Remember playing tug of war as a child? As long as the parties on each end of the rope are tugging, you have a 'war.' But when someone lets go, the war is over. When you forgive . . . you are letting go of your end of the rope. No matter how hard he may tug on the other end, if you have released your end, the war is over for you."[1]

WHAT FORGIVENESS IS NOT

Laura found out about Phil's first affair after they'd been married less than a year. He had tried to hide the evidence, but Laura was a bright woman, and confronted him with motel charges and phone bills.

In tears, and with deep regret, Phil asked Laura to forgive him. "Darling," he said, his voiced choked with emotion, "I'll make it up to you. I was weak, but I'm going to be strong. Please . . . give me another chance."

Laura is a Christian who believes that forgiveness is an important part of her faith. When Phil apologized, she summoned all her inner strength and said, "I love you, Phil. Let's try to work through this."

Before another year had passed, motel charges were again turning up on their American Express statements. Someone was calling and hanging up when Laura answered the phone. Phil was staying out unusually late some nights and seemed overly loving and attentive when he came in.

Finally, Laura could deny the obvious no longer. She confronted him. "Phil, it's happening again, isn't it?"

Again Phil asked for forgiveness. And, again, Laura forgave him. This pattern became as familiar a part of their marriage as their faithful churchgoing. Through it all, Phil attended Sunday services with Laura, wore his best smile, and cried in all the right places during convicting sermons.

After ten years of unending marital unfaithfulness, with the full approval of her parents, her friends, and her pastor, Laura asked Phil to move out.

"Laura!" Phil stammered in disbelief. "I thought you were a Christian! I cannot imagine how a Christian can refuse to forgive and forget. You know I'm sorry. You know I love you. What on earth would make you want to separate from me. Laura, darling, you aren't thinking of divorce, are you?"

IT IS NOT FORGETTING, IGNORING, DENYING, OR PRETENDING

God wants us to be "wise as serpents, and harmless as doves" (Matthew 10:16 KJV). That means that we need to learn who is trustworthy and who is not. (We'll talk more about trustworthy people in the next chapter.) Obviously Laura's narcissistic and sexually addicted husband was not a safe person, worthy of her trust. And as long as she offered him cheap forgiveness, he would continue his wayward behavior.

IT IS NOT ACQUITTAL

Acquittal says that the person didn't commit the sin in the first place. Somehow the offender wasn't responsible. Acquittal lies about pain, and it requires denial—the person injured must act as if the hurt never happened. This is a manifestation of the powerless love position. Forgiveness, on the other hand, is equivalent to offering the person who injured you a pardon. A pardon acknowledges that the injury occurred but states that there is no penalty for the sin.

IT IS NOT RECONCILIATION

Forgiveness is strictly personal—it goes on inside me. Reconciliation is different. It includes the other person, requiring him (or her) to be involved in the same forgiving process that I am in, leading toward a fully restored relationship. It is important to keep in mind that when you forgive someone, you may be the only person healed. What the other person does about his relationship with you is beyond your control.

IT IS NOT INSTANTANEOUS—IT IS A PROCESS

Forgiveness always begins with a decision to free ourselves from chains of bitterness and revenge even though we may not necessarily "feel like it" at the moment. Forgiveness means that we choose to walk toward grace, freedom, and peace of mind.

C. S. Lewis was badly hurt by a teacher who exemplified the loveless power stance. The teacher was a sadist who turned the lives of the boys in an English private school into living hell. For most of his life, Lewis struggled with forgiving him. A few months before his death, in a letter to an American friend, Lewis talked about a change that had taken place in his attitude to that teacher.

> Dear Mary,
>
> . . . Do you know, only a few weeks ago I realized suddenly that I had at last forgiven the cruel schoolmaster who so darkened my childhood. I'd been trying to do it for years; and like you, each time I thought I'd done it, I found, after a week or so, it all had to be attempted over again. But this time I feel sure it is the real thing . . .
>
> Yours,
>
> Jack[2]

Even though I may have chosen to take the route that leads to forgiveness, I will still have to work through the emotional consequences of the wrong done to me. There will be pain, resentment, and confusion. But the process of forgiveness has a clearly miraculous quality. Not only are you freed when I offer you forgiveness, but I also am set free. After a period of time the hurt will no longer affect my relationship with you. I will remember it and will have to deal with the consequences of it, but it will no longer own my soul. I will have "put it down," as the monk said.

Along the Pathway of Forgiveness

Even though we are in the process of forgiving, we may still feel angry or hurt when we recall a painful act. That is because when we forgive we do not change the facts and we do not forget. As a consequence, sometimes when we recall the event we will experience an emotional response to it. The fact is, anger and hate do not have to be synonymous. Anger can be a positive emotion, in the sense that it spurs us to prevent the wrong from happening again. When wisely invested in necessary precautions, anger can bring hope—hope for a better, safer relationship.

Understanding a little of what it was like for the other person will aid us in our progress. Understanding helps us forgive but should not cause us to excuse or tolerate wrongful hurts. The offender could have opted for other choices. Forgiveness has begun when you recall those who have hurt you and acknowledge that they have done you wrong; notwithstanding, you feel a sense of empathy and find the energy to wish them well.

Sometimes forgiveness is risky business. It involves making ourselves vulnerable. People may say, "You're a fool! Look at what he did to you. I'd never forgive him." It is helpful to remember that forgiveness is for our good. When we go into surgery, we allow a team of physicians to cut us. We are at their mercy while we are under anesthesia. Why? Because it is an acceptable risk to make us more healthy. So it is with forgiveness.

SEEKING OTHERS' FORGIVENESS

The Bible clearly connects our forgiveness of others with our own need to be forgiven. Jesus taught us to pray, "Forgive us our trespasses as we forgive those who trespass against us." While we are making ourselves aware of people we should forgive, we ought also to consider those against whom we may have sinned. In working through the process of repentance and asking forgiveness ourselves, we will learn valuable lessons about granting forgiveness to others.

Asking to be forgiven is difficult, humbling, but very healthy. Here are some helpful steps necessary for moving into repentance.

- Own the truth that you have injured others.
  - Make a list of the people you have hurt
  - Next to each name write the injury you inflicted.
  - Carefully reread what you just wrote. Is it defensive? Are you trying to explain yourself? Are you making excuses?
- Decide to take responsibility to repair the injury.
  Do this by contacting the individuals in person, by writing a letter, or by making contact by telephone.
- Admit your wrongdoing and ask for forgiveness.
  David Viscott provides suggestions for asking forgiveness. In his book *Emotionally Free,* he suggests that the ideal message will contain a selection of the following points:
  - "I'm sorry I hurt your feelings when I acted the way I did."
  - "I was selfish and didn't care about anyone else at the time but myself."
  - "I acted out of greed and fear."
  - "I was not at my best."
  - "I've often thought about how I hurt you, and it has caused me pain."
  - "I want you to know that I haven't forgotten, that I've suffered in recalling my unfortunate actions."

- "I wish I could take back what I said or did, but I can't. What has happened lives in me as discomfort."
- "I know I can't make your pain go away, but I hope you understand that I'm deeply sorry."
- "Please accept my apologies."
- "Please forgive me."
- "I wish you the best."
- "I want you to forgive me for my imperfections and short-comings."
- "I want you to forgive me for failing you."[3]

If the person chooses to express the hurt he has felt, do not become defensive and attempt to justify yourself. Do not make excuses. Listen. Thank the other person for expressing his pain. Allow his truth to be spoken, even if it makes you feel uncomfortable, misunderstood, or insecure.

Many of us find accepting an apology more difficult than giving an apology. It takes truth ("Yes, I was deeply hurt when you did _____") and grace ("I forgive you because God has done that for me"). The choice to accept an apology is not sentimental, condescending, manipulative, or conditional.

I FORGIVE BECAUSE I WANT TO BE HEALTHY

Of course we are people with a free will. We have the right to withhold forgiveness if we choose. But to accept an apology is wise—not only for the good of the offender or even for our good, but because it pleases God.

God's Word requires forgiveness from God's people. Perhaps this is so because He knows that whatever I have not forgiven still controls me. Revenge boomerangs back on the revenger. Corrie ten Boom is quoted as saying, "To forgive is to set a prisoner free and to find out that prisoner is me." The reason to forgive others is not to let them off the hook, but to free ourselves from the burden of hating.

Unforgiveness is a dangerous choice. The longer we hate, the more damaging it is to us personally. We can move from being a person who hides hatred inside, to being a person who acts in hatred. Rather than our hate belonging to us, we belong to it. Before long, our hate becomes our future, affecting our behavior, our thinking, even our physical health.

Lewis B. Smedes says, "We attach our feelings to the moment when we were hurt, endowing it with immortality. And we let it assault us every time it comes to mind. It travels with us, sleeps with us, hovers over us while we make love, and broods over us while we die. Our hate does not even have the decency to die when those we hate die, for it is a parasite sucking our blood, not theirs."[4]

People who forgive get well. Those who do not, don't; and we cannot have it both ways. When I choose not to forgive, there are consequences.

- I am guided by my anger, pain, and hatred.
- I am directed by my negative memories.
- I am full of the abusing person.
- I do not act freely.
- I attempt to control situations and people to keep the offense from happening to me again.
- I live with tension and stress as my constant companions.
- My relationship with God is empty.
- My relationship with myself is strained.
- My relationship with others is guarded.
- My life span is probably reduced.

I FORGIVE BECAUSE I NEED TO BE FORGIVEN

We are both good and bad. The Bible teaches that we are, on the one hand, made in the image of God. On the other hand, God says that our hearts are continuously evil. This is not a Biblical contradiction, but a fact of life. We are both good news and bad news. No matter who we are or what great things we may have accomplished, we are all weak, needy, imperfect human beings. It is realistic and necessary for us to see ourselves and others as being some good, and some not so good.

Lewis B. Smedes says:

> We are seldom merely sinned against. We often contribute to our own vulnerability. We set ourselves up for hurt. Sometimes we invite pain, not because we love somebody too much, but because we are too stupid. Maybe we contribute to our being ripped-off because we are too lazy to look hard before we leap into a deal. Maybe we contribute to our spouses' infidelity by our unfeeling ignorance of his or her needs and desires. Maybe we contribute to our children's rebellion by our cold judgments and hot tempers. Surely we know at least this much, that even if we are the hurt party, we are seldom a completely innocent party. Our virtue is always compromised; we are never as innocent as we feel when we taste our early hate for a person who has hurt us.[5]

As we forgive, we are in the process of learning to love what is real—both the good and the bad—in ourselves and others. God sought total relationship rather than simply associating Himself with our "good" side. That choice led Him to His crucifixion. "While we were still sinners, Christ died for us" (Romans 5:8).

It is easy for us to be committed to an idealized concept of a person. But when we forgive, we recommit ourselves to an imperfect, flawed person. The reality of good and bad has been exposed. It is a physical demonstration on earth of what God has done for us even though we have repeatedly betrayed Him.

When we forgive a person, we commit to work on ourselves and not on the other person. We leave it up to God to work with others with regard to their various imperfections.

- Forgiveness frees us from judgment and from the role of judge.
- Forgiveness frees others from our scrutiny.
- Forgiveness lets go in order to let others go on.
- Forgiveness is a great liberator when it becomes a central element of our lifestyle.

I
am.
I am I.
I am one.
I am many.
I am a community
of persons known, loved, hated.
Within me lives a collection of people
I have followed or fought, accepted or avoided,
chosen as good models, rejected as bad models,
prized, valued, idealized and/or disliked, devalued, despised.
They are all there, remembered or forgotten somewhere within.
I have grown from their gifts, good or bad.
I have gained much because they were there.
They are my teachers, my guides.
They make up my museum,
my inner community,
my community
of the spirit.
Because of
them all
I am
I.[6]

Along similar lines, forgiving ourselves is imperative. If I don't expect myself to be perfect, I don't hate myself when I'm not. If I don't expect to be in complete control, I won't blame myself when things go awry. When I forgive myself and others I am taking personal responsibility for my needs, body, and choices. Self-forgiveness is an act of faith, in which I receive and appropriate God's forgiveness. In doing so, I release myself from my own self-judgment and self-punishment.

I FORGIVE BECAUSE GOD HAS FORGIVEN ME

"For if you forgive men when they sin against you, your heavenly Father will also forgive you. But if you do not forgive men their sins, your Father will not forgive your sins" (Matthew 6:14–15).

When we accept God's forgiveness we are moving from a "should" system to a grace system. We do not want to be judged on the basis of a "should" system. None of us wants to reap what we deserve.

David Stoop and James Masteller have this to say about forgiveness:

> Forgiveness is important for God's sake. Every wrong is an offense first and foremost against a wise and loving God who does not wish to see any of his creatures harmed and who "takes it personally" when they are wronged. . . . An important part of our being able to work out our own forgiveness is drawn from the forgiveness that God himself has shown us.[7]

Ephesians 4:32 says, "Be kind and compassionate to one another, forgiving each other, just as in Christ God forgave you."

Colossians 3:13 says, "Bear with each other and forgive whatever grievances you may have against one another. Forgive as the Lord forgave you."

God is, and always was, the first forgiver. Because He has forgiven me, I can willingly begin the process of forgiving those who have wronged me. The question is not whether the other person deserves forgiveness. The question is, How will I respond to God's grace?

After an adulterous woman anointed His feet with perfume, kissed them, and wiped them with her repentant tears, Jesus told a story. Two men owed money to a loan shark. One owed fifty coins, the other five hundred. The loan shark decided to forgive the debt.

"Now," Jesus asked, "which of these two men will love him more?"

Simon, a self-righteous Pharisee, answered, "I suppose the one who had the bigger debt canceled."

Simon was correct. Jesus affirmed him, but went on to point out a further truth.

Jesus had spent the evening as an invited dinner guest in Simon's home. Unfortunately, although Simon was the host, he had not bothered to wash Jesus' feet, a common courtesy of the time. Neither had Simon greeted Jesus with a kiss or put oil on His head. The adulterous woman, in her unique way, had taken care of all three kindnesses. Jesus words to Simon are piercing. "Therefore, I tell you, her many sins have been forgiven—for she loved much. But he who has been forgiven little loves little" (Luke 7:41–48).

Like the woman's costly perfume, God's mercy has been lavishly poured out on all of us. Can we recognize it, receive it and let it motivate us to be grace-givers? You will never have to forgive anyone for more than God has forgiven you. Besides, forgiveness is the only way the grace of God and the love of people will ever get inside us. Forgiveness makes way for the restoration of relationships.

"When you are praying, first forgive anyone you are holding a grudge against, so that your Father in heaven will forgive you your sins too" (Mark 11:25 TLB).

According to God's unique economy, we can never receive what we are not willing to give.

LOVELESS POWER AND FORGIVENESS

When the issue between two people is one of power or control, the act of forgiveness becomes complicated by the characteristics of those involved in the offense. The controller's automatic defense in all situations is to blame other factors or people for his mistakes. Because of his (or her) habit of making excuses, he cannot admit to his mistakes and therefore cannot learn from them. This person relies on excuses and blame to superimpose external order on the world and, in doing so, cleverly conceals his own self-doubt. Asking for forgiveness never occurs to him.

The controller will use any tool he or she can invent to sidestep vulnerability. Only lip service is given to remorse. Inflexibility, rationalization, projection, and blaming are the well-worn, overused tools these individuals constantly utilize.

Controllers

- Tend to forgive too slowly
- Don't take responsibility
- Live a waiting life
- Allow a root of bitterness to spring up
- Adopt the victim's role
- Rationalize and excuse their own shortcomings
- Are terrified of personal vulnerability
- Crave sympathy

Sometimes Christian controllers find a unique, "spiritual" way to avoid true forgiveness. As David Augsburger says, "When 'forgiveness' puts you one-up, on top in a superior place as the benefactor, the generous one, the giver of freedom and dignity, don't trust it. Don't give it. Don't accept it. It is not forgiveness; it's sweet, saintly revenge."[8]

In order to mature we have to take our eyes off what other people do or don't do. Our challenge is to look at ourselves, take responsibility, risk, and act.

POWERLESS LOVE AND FORGIVENESS

Whereas the controller places blame, the powerless lover's tendency is to use denial to protect himself (or herself) against abandonment, the loss of love, or the risk of injury. This defense originates early in life—a helpless child uses it to shut out pain. Unfortunately, continually using denial to deal with life's realities obscures problems, rendering them impossible to solve. Naturally, this aggravates feelings of helplessness and hopelessness.

Dependents

- Forgive too quickly (cheap forgiveness means excusing)
- Deny the hurt—"It wasn't that bad"
- Take on too much of the responsibility
- Retreat instead of saying "You sinned against me," or "You injured me"

FORGIVENESS

LOVELESS POWER	POWERFUL LOVE	POWERLESS LOVE
Shifts responsibility	Takes responsibility	Excuses responsibility
Acts in response to injury	Feels the injury	Denies injury
Wants revenge	Wants truth/reality/ relationship	Wants peace
Never forgets	Remembers but can bless	Denies and blesses
Tolerates nothing	Refuses to tolerate injustice and evil	Tolerates everything
Hate focused on a person	Hate focused on an action	What hate?
Betrays others	Wants truth	Covers up for others
Confronts the person's character	Confronts the action that led to injury	Avoids confrontation

THE PROCESS OF FORGIVENESS

How do we learn to forgive? Like anything else in life, we do not master forgiveness by taking one giant step from hate into love. We move forward little by little. And we begin, as we always do in any new endeavor, by taking that all-important first step.

Step #1. I acknowledge that I have been injured.

This process begins when we feel some kind of pain or hurt or when a wrong has been done to us. Journaling is incredibly important here. Write down what happened, who was involved, and the effect it had on you. What got broken? Was it your ability to trust? Was it your right to set limits? Was it your ability to take responsibility?

Step #2. I own the feelings associated with the injuries.

Just as God has given us an immune system to fight dangerous infections, so He has given each of us a grieving system to help us deal with the losses and disappointments of life. We must freely feel our emotions in order to energize this system to do its work.

This step is a challenging one, because many of us do not take responsibility for our own feelings. Often when we are asked what our *feelings* are, we respond by telling people what we *think*. Not dealing with our feelings in the forgiveness process causes us to practice denial. There are a number of emotions that result from injury.

Fear is commonly associated with past childhood injuries or with continuing threats to body, soul, or spirit.

Guilt has to do with wrongs we believe we have committed.

Shame is a sense that we are somehow flawed, and it makes us want to isolate for fear that "the truth about us" will come out and people will reject us.

Anger often indicates too many demands and expectations. This may result from overtly imposed control or criticism, or from smothering and overprotection.

Hurt in relationships often stems from too little attention, appreciation, approval, or affection. Everyone of us feels hurt in relationships at one time or another.

Owning our feelings is a painful process. It sometimes helps to "fill in the blanks," saying,

- I am afraid of _____ .
- I feel guilty about _____ .
- I feel shame because of _____ .
- I felt embarrassed when _____ .
- I am angry that _____ .
- I was hurt by _____ .
- I was disappointed when _____ .

Step #3. I express my feelings, especially the anger and hurt I feel toward someone else.

Grace always comes to us from the outside. It comes from God Himself and from safe, grace-giving relationships in which we are assured of complete confidentiality. God's Word tells us that we need to be rooted and grounded in love.

If we stay in isolation with our feelings, there is only one person living in our heart—the person who hurt us. It is humbling to say to a caring person, "I need you," "I'm frightened," "I'm hurt."

In 1 John 1:9 we are told that confession is a prerequisite to healing. Confession means that we agree with the truth. Bring the truth to someone who is safe—a person who won't condemn you, moralize, shame you, or share your truth with others.

Other than talking, there are alternatives in this process.

- We can write a letter that we don't intend to send, expressing our truth to the person who has offended us.
- We can journal.
- We can talk into a tape recorder.

Regardless of which method you choose, move out of isolation and toward trustworthy people with your truth. Expose your pain to the light of another's insight and understanding.

Step #4. I abandon my need for revenge.

Forgiveness is not about good people forgiving bad people or innocent people forgiving guilty people. Forgiveness is about sinners forgiving sinners. Vengeance belongs to God. It is not my job. My job is to set myself free through the process of forgiveness.

Step #5. I accept forgiveness from God for my part in the problem, if I had a part.

"If we confess our sins, He is faithful and just and will forgive us our sins and purify us from all unrighteousness" (1 John 1:9).

"As far as the east is from the west, so far has he removed our transgressions from us" (Psalm 103:12).

Obviously a child who is sexually or physically abused by an adult is not to blame in any way for the adult's choices. But as adults involved in relationships, we do have choices. Perhaps, for example, your spouse had an affair. You feel sinned against, and you are. Yet it is possible that you may have sinned against your spouse somewhere along the way. Reflect on the sin against you. What did you do to contribute to the problem?

Step #6. I take personal responsibility for setting and communicating my boundaries.

In their book *Boundaries,* Henry Cloud and John Townsend give two illustrations of the difference between nagging and setting boundaries.

Before Boundaries	After Boundaries
1. "Stop yelling at me. You must be nicer."	1. "You can continue to yell if you choose to. But I will choose not to be in your presence when you act that way."
2. "You've just got to stop drinking. It's ruining our family. Please listen. You're wrecking our lives."	2. "You may choose to not deal with your drinking if you want. But I will not continue to expose myself and the children to this chaos. The next time you are drunk, we will go to the Wilson's for the night, and we will tell them why we are there. Your drinking is your choice. What I will put up with is mine."[9]

We are responsible for our bodies, attitudes, behavior, thoughts, abilities, wants, choices, beliefs, limits (what we will and will not put up with), and our "No!" boundaries allow us to get close to another person without fear of invasion. If we take responsibility for someone else, we stifle their growth and neglect our own. If we don't take responsibility for ourselves by setting boundaries and communicating them, we are ultimately responsible for the wrongs that are done against us.

Step #7. I approach the other person with forgiveness, using the tools mentioned earlier in the chapter.

Step #8. If I choose, I approach the person with the possibility of reconciliation.

"If your brother sins against you, go and show him his fault, just between the two of you. If he listens to you, you have won your brother over" (Matthew 18:15).

If the other person chooses not to reconcile, we still choose to forgive. We are set free, but we will have to grieve the loss of a relationship,

If we are alive and breathing, someone has hurt us along the way—it is a given. It is just as inevitable that we have hurt others, whether we meant to or not. But no matter what injuries we may have suffered, for our present and future health and happiness, we shall resolve the following:

- Let's learn how to bond again.
- Let's set limits again, making detached self-protectiveness unnecessary.
- Let's be active, not passive.
- Let's move toward the risk of relationship and out of the safety of isolation.
- Let's love again, overthrowing our hatred.
- Let's freely give and freely receive forgiveness.
- Let's find a way to stretch ourselves beyond our bitterness, our fear, and our solitude.
- Let's allow God to teach us to forgive one another

How tenderly He has loved and forgiven us!

Notes

1. H. Norman Wright, *Always Daddy's Girl* (Ventura, Calif.: Regal, 1989, 235–36.
2. C. S. Lewis, quoted in Lewis B. Smedes, *Forgive and Forget: Healing the Hurts We Don't Deserve* (San Francisco: Harper & Row, 1984), 95.
3. David Viscott, M.D., *Emotionally Free* (Chicago: Contemporary Books, 1992), 250–53.
4. Smedes, 23.
5. Ibid., 147–48.
6. David Augsburger, *Caring Enough to Forgive/Not to Forgive* (Ventura, Calif.: Regal, 1981), 81. Used by permission.
7. David Stoop, M.D., and James Masteller, M.D., *Forgiving Our Parents, Forgiving Ourselves* (Ann Arbor, Mich.: Servant, 1991), 161.

8. Augsburger, 8.

9. Henry Cloud and John Townsend, *Boundaries* (Grand Rapids: Zondervan, 1992), 157.

9

PERSONAL POWER IN CRISIS

Donna was walking along the beach, lost in thought. She was deeply hurt, and her steps in the sand were slow. The man she'd loved for years had found another lover. She'd just found out the day before, and her thoughts were still a muddle of shock, rejection, and disbelief.

Yesterday morning, Donna had lightheartedly driven up to Kevin's apartment, carrying two croissants and two steaming cups of coffee. She hadn't called first—she wanted to surprise him. As it turned out, Donna was the one who was in for a surprise.

When she knocked on Kevin's door, a slender, brown-eyed woman opened it. She was carelessly wrapped in a bathrobe, and it was obvious she had just gotten out of bed—Kevin's bed. Donna had become hysterical. After an angry scene, she'd told Kevin to get out of her life and stay out.

But, as she walked along the sea, listening to the cries of gulls and the soothing rhythm of the waves, she knew that before long it would be up to her to keep Kevin away once and for all. She knew, in the clarity her present heartbreak had given her, that Kevin was a user. He'd taken her money, her time, her attention, her food. She'd rescued him more times than she could remember—she had even bailed him out of jail a couple of times. And Kevin had given nothing in return. Kevin seemed strangely unable to love. He had no problem making love, which he did very well. But as far as love itself was concerned, Kevin was only able to receive. He was either unable or unwilling to give.

Donna began to pray, silently and sadly. Why would God listen to her? She'd been breaking some of His most well-known rules. She had sinned. She had gotten burned. Nevertheless she whispered, "God, why do I make such stupid mistakes? Why do I always get hurt?"

As she walked, she noticed two or three honeybees that were lying right at the surf's edge, trapped in the sand and water. She carefully stepped over them, not wanting their stingers in her bare feet. Then, after walking a few more yards, she saw a monarch butterfly struggling in the sand. She quickly scooped it up, brushed it off and carried it across the beach to some plants, where she left it to dry.

Donna chuckled to herself. *Always the rescuer,* she thought. *I never learn.*

Then into her mind came a very clear thought. "My child, you were wise not to pick up the bees—they will always sting you—that's their nature. If you would be as wise with people as you are with insects, you wouldn't get hurt. Only pick up the ones that don't have stingers, child. Leave the others to me."

"Thanks Lord," Donna whispered with tears in her eyes. "I guess You heard me after all."

The most valuable assets we have in a crisis are our friends and our faith. As Donna learned in the midst of her own personal crisis, choosing trustworthy people to love can prevent some of our worst heartbreaks. And knowing who to turn to in our pain also requires wisdom. Later in the chapter, we'll talk about trustworthy people. But first, let's take a look at some difficulties and challenges we may face. And let's develop tools we can use to cope with them.

THE TIMES THAT TRY OUR SOULS

There is no one time in life when we need God more than another. *All* of life is an ongoing process of getting to know the Lord—learning to love Him, learning to count on Him. But there are circumstances in life that we call crises. Those are the times we cry out to Him in panic and cling to the slender thread of our faith with both hands. How do we define a crisis? To give you an idea as to what the psychological community identifies as high anxiety situations, take a look at the Holmes-Rahe Stress Test.

In addition to these factors, which can affect anyone, there are ten predictable crises that occur in courtship and marriage. When we are emotionally involved with another person, those circumstances also require the summoning of all our resources. They confront us with our worst fears of abandonment, rejection, absorption, and loss of control.

1. *Falling in love.* Two people meet, date, and enter a fantasy stage. Infatuation reigns supreme, and the first crisis occurs only if one person panics and retreats.

2. *Engagement "cold feet."* Prior to either the engagement or wedding one party may withdraw (usually the man), perhaps because of fear that he will lose himself. The wedding is often a peak experience in a woman's life; it is a lesser event for a man.

3. *Marriage-is-a-real-eye-opener.* Love may be blind but marriage isn't. After six months to a year, infatuation dwindles and lovers have their eyes wide open. The partners have to acknowledge that they each married a fantasy of their own making. At this stage they have to get to know and learn to live with the real person.

HOLMES-RAHE STRESS TEST

In the past 12 months, which of these have happened to you?

EVENT	VALUE	SCORE	EVENT	VALUE	SCORE
Death of spouse	100	___	Son or daughter		
Divorce	73	___	leaving home	29	___
Marital separation	65	___	Trouble with in-laws	29	___
Jail term	63	___	Outstanding personal		
Death of close			achievement	28	___
family member	63	___	Spouse begins or		
Personal injury			starts work	26	___
or illness	53	___	Starting or finishing		
Marriage	50	___	school	26	___
Fired from work	47	___	Change in living		
Marital reconciliation	45	___	conditions	25	___
Retirement	45	___	Revision of personal		
Change in family			habits	24	___
member's health	44	___	Trouble with boss	23	___
Pregnancy	40	___	Change in work hours,		
Sex difficulties	39	___	conditions	20	___
Addition to family	39	___	Change in residence	20	___
Business readjustment	39	___	Change in schools	20	___
Change in financial			Change in recreational		
status	38	___	habits	19	___
Death of close friend	37	___	Change in church activities	19	___
Change in number of			Change in social activities	18	___
marital arguments	35	___	Mortgage or loan under		
Mortgage or loan			$10,000	18	___
over $10,000	31	___	Change in sleeping habits	16	___
Foreclosure or			Change in number of		
mortgage or loan	30	___	family gatherings	15	___
Change in work			Change in eating habits	15	___
responsibilities	29	___	Vacation	13	___
			Christmas season	12	___
			Minor violation of the law	11	___
			TOTAL		___

Total your score

0–150 = Low Stress
150–300 = Average Stress
Over 300 = High Stress

This test measures stress due to situational changes.

Reprinted with permission of T. H. Holmes and R. H. Rahe, "The Social Adjustment Rating Scale," *Journal of Psychosomatic Research* 2:213. Copyright 1967, Pergamon Press.

4. *Family ties.* Men and women equally share the challenge of adjusting to each others' families. Clashes and rivalries can develop. To make matters worse, ex-spouses and stepchildren complicate the picture enormously.

5. *That first child.* Becoming parents changes each spouse's view of the other. They are now parents, not honeymooners. If they still carry emotional baggage from their family of origin, it will now be unpacked, revealing previously unseen characteristics. All this happens in the face of much added responsibility.

6. *The thrill is gone.* Eventually sex becomes a less passionate sport. Typically the man experiences sexual decline and the wife blames herself for this reality.

7. *Is that all there is?* Couples begin to focus less on career accomplishments and more on their personal relationship—or vice versa. It is easy to pass one another at this stage.

8. *Older and wiser.* Each spouse becomes aware that the other is growing older. This amounts to a less threatening way of acknowledging one's own aging process. In the midst of this, grown children are often summoned to care for elderly parents. Traditionally, the lion's share of this responsibility falls on the wife's shoulders.

9. *The empty nest.* As children leave home, husbands and wives are no longer distracted from the realities of their marriage. They must face each other on their own. If the wife's identity has been invested in being a mother, she may now turn to her husband for emotional attachment. If he is unresponsive, she might start a career or search for other diversions.

10. *Those final years.* The trauma of this stage is greatly increased when the two people age at different speeds, or one spouse dies. Here individuals try to accept their failures and successes without despair or pre-

occupation with what might have been. Impending death becomes an actuality, and relationships become more important that ever.

How each of us deals with these crises depends on our personality, character, and maturity. Are you one who controls with loveless power? Are you a dependent who acts in powerless love? Or are you moving into a place of powerful love, with Christ as your example? Let's take a look at how each type of person might react to some common crisis.

WHAT IF SOMEONE YOU LOVE LEAVES YOU?

If a loved one threatens to move on, the loveless power player will probably pursue, badger, block the other's exit, manipulate, demand, reason, and make excuses. If that doesn't work, he (or she) might choose to communicate that the other person really didn't matter anyway.

The powerless lover will respond frantically, pleading, begging, clinging. After all, his (or her) identity is wrapped up in the other and, therefore, is about to be lost.

If we are powerful lovers, we own our hurt and sadness, and try to communicate with the other person in an attempt to gain understanding. Ultimately, if reconciliation fails, we accept the decision and seek closure. We are left in the house of mourning.

WHAT IF YOUR MOST IMPORTANT PROJECT COLLAPSES?

When a pet project starts to crumble, a controller will probably embark on a great cover-up, pushing harder than ever to employ the very strategy that has failed. Rigidity increases. The controller fears showing any weakness, so he (or she) points a finger at everybody else and blames them. Some individuals may pretend that everything has turned out just the way it was supposed to. "I saw this coming," they'll say with a wise nod.

The dependent will probably panic. If he (or she) has made a mistake, he will begin to see his entire existence as a mistake. Anticipating rejection, the powerless lover blindly seeks affirmation and support anywhere he can get it.

The powerful lover's stance would be to face the problem head-on. We might reexamine our presuppositions, our goals, and our procedures. We will want to know what went wrong so we can avoid the same problem in the future.

WHAT IF YOU HAVE HURT SOMEONE CLOSE TO YOU?

A wife, a parent, or a child sits weeping, deeply grieved by the behavior of a loved one. How does that loved one respond? How would you respond?

A person who practices loveless power may direct accusations at the injured person and set out to prove how well-deserved the hurt was. If that won't work, he (or she) will pretend that the incident was an accident, or say, "Oh, c'mon! I was only kidding. Can't you take a joke?"

The powerless lover will apologize profusely. He (or she) will review the infraction a thousand times, berating himself, more terrorized at the thought of losing the loved one's love than sorry for the hurt itself.

As powerful lovers, we will express remorse and take responsibility for the hurt. We will say "I'm sorry," ask forgiveness, and refrain from repeating the hurt.

WHAT IF YOU FIND YOURSELF
PASSED OVER FOR A PROMOTION?

The job of your dreams has been up for grabs for months. This morning you were called into the boss's office and informed that the position is going to someone else. What do you do?

If you're a controller, you'll probably try to get even. You may become preoccupied with creating a "plan" to undo the wrong. Paranoia may surface along with obstructive and vindictive behavior. Some controllers choose to quit the company altogether, impulsively saying "I don't need this job anyway."

Powerless lovers will gather support to validate their belief that they have been treated unfairly. They will feel worthless and be convinced that they will never amount to anything.

As powerful lovers, we will reevaluate our performance. We'll attempt to learn from this unpleasant experience. Perhaps we will request a job review, while questioning and examining our own methods. We own our disappointment but would use the disappointment to spur us on towards our goal.

WHAT IF YOUR CHILD IS A SENIOR
IN HIGH SCHOOL ANTICIPATING COLLEGE?

Junior is trying to figure out what he wants to be when he grows up. Mom and Dad are nervously watching this process, acting and reacting according to their personalities.

A controlling parent may order the child to go to the college of that parent's choice. "That's the only way I'm paying for your education," the parent will tell his son or daughter. Or the parent may increase control in other areas, perhaps in areas such as criticism or in exerting control over friendships or curfews.

The powerless lover will likely spend the senior year sadly telling the child how much value and meaning he gives the parents. He (or she) will plead with the child to attend a college that is extremely close to home. There may be tearful scenes and sorrowful regrets expressed. "I just haven't been a good enough parent. I should have done more."

If we are parents who are powerful lovers, we will have spent the last eighteen-odd years preparing our child to leave home. This effort will have accelerated during the course of the senior year. We will provide the child with opportunities and allow him (or her) to make the majority of his own decisions. We will make ourselves available to discuss options and to help set goals. If our child makes some poor choices along the way, we will accept him personally, but will allow him to experience the consequences of his decisions.

WHAT LOSSES REVEAL ABOUT POWER VS. LOVE

When losses of any kind arise, their impact upon us will depend on our tendency toward control, dependency, or interdependence. Loveless power individuals operate on the premise that they must try to control the love of others. In childhood, they either lost a parent's love attachment, or a parent's power turned against them in some way. They made a "never again" commitment at that time.

Controllers are deeply affected by the loss of power, position, influence, seniority, authority, or access to those sources of power. They fear the loss of money, work, financial status, and success, as well as the loss of physical strength, youth, and health. They also suffer greatly at the loss of reputation, image, and social or professional standing.

When powerless lovers—dependents—have losses, they are symbolic of the loss of a parent's love and therefore trigger a sense of helplessness, hopelessness, and powerlessness. Dependents may question their ability even to survive. Until they have completed their mourning over childhood losses, adult losses will compel them into a bottomless pit of depression, helplessness, and powerlessness.

Losses the powerless lovers will particularly mourn include the loss of a person, the loss of a person's love, the loss of self, or the loss of any belief in personal lovableness.

In her landmark book *Questions and Answers on Death and Dying*[1] Elisabeth Kubler-Ross describes five stages of grief most people experience after the loss of a loved one. If the crisis you are going through involves a loss of any kind, these stages will apply to you.

STAGE ONE: DENIAL

LOVELESS POWER

Go immediately into action
   to escape pain (sense of
   power)
Detach, become superficial

POWERLESS LOVE

Deny pain for as long as
   possible
Fluctuate between horror of
   knowing and anxiety of
   accepting

STAGE TWO: DEPRESSION

Keep busy to avoid pain
Obsess over minutiae
Preoccupation with thoughts
   rather than feelings

Self-pity, loss of life's meaning
Self-condemnation, regret
Catastrophic thinking

STAGE THREE: ANGER

Wants revenge/a vendetta
Blames others while hiding
   self-accusing thoughts
Isolates, becomes closed
   and tough

Poor me, the victim
Displaces anger
Panic attacks
Isolates, becomes immobilized

STAGE FOUR: BARGAINING

Fights back tears to appear
   in control
Scolds other for displaying
   emotion
Tries to control God with
   bargaining

Analyzes loss and reasons for it
Pleads and begs for God to
   change reality

STAGE FIVE: ACCEPTANCE

Fights feelings of vulnerability
"Never again!"
Stays busy and reestablishes
   control in tasks

Yearns for what was lost
Lives in resignation and fear

DEALING IN THE EXTREMES

When a painful loss is not worked through, it persists as sorrow, as a nostalgic or angry state, or as a fear. An unmourned loss deeply influences our present as well as our future. We all have to face disappointments and anger when life doesn't work out the way we expect it to. A crisis is no time to set priorities or to form a value system. A crisis reveals our true colors.

When the world is collapsing around us, we run to the familiar—the response patterns that we used as children and saw modeled for us by adult authority figures. Stop and think. What were your patterns of dealing with frustration as a youngster? Did you get loud and verbally aggressive? Did you come out fighting? Did you weep and withdraw? Did you pretend nothing had happened and escape into a fantasy world?

We revert to our weakness, and our weakness is either the understating or overstating of our strengths. In times of difficulty, we often deal in the extremes. Overstating strengths occurs when we feel rigid and self-protective. Understating strengths occurs when we wish to be compliant and avoid conflict.

OVERSTATE	STRENGTH	UNDERSTATE
Don't let others in	Openness	Too Open
Dishonesty	Honesty	Too honest
Withholding	Giving	Martyr
Suspicious	Trusting	Gullible
(Loveless Power)	(Powerful Love)	(Powerless Love)

THE SECRET CRISIS: PHYSICAL ABUSE

The ultimate example of loveless power is physical abuse. Child and spousal battering have reached epidemic levels in the United States, and therapists' offices are full to overflowing with stories of out-of-control anger that has erupted into violence. Perhaps you or someone you love is trapped in a situation where beatings and bruises are the most compelling form of communication.

If so, remember that most battered wives are caught in a constant crisis—a cycle of attack and apology, rage and repentance. These women are usually convinced by their violent partners that they are responsible for the problem. They aren't good enough wives. They don't clean house perfectly. They "flirt" with other men. They don't "obey" their husbands as strictly as they should. The list of excuses for violence include just about anything. Of course there is no defense of such behavior, but battered women are afraid to leave because of guilt, threats, humiliation, financial constraints and, sadly, even because of religious convictions and misunderstanding.

Recent articles in southern California newspapers report that wife beating is quite widespread in many fundamentalist and authoritarian churches, churches that sometimes stress male supremacy and wifely submission. The *Orange County Register*[2] offered an interesting profile of an abusive man.

A man is considered likely to abuse a woman if he

- Lacks self-esteem
- Is a traditionalist
- Is emotionally inexpressive
- Is unassertive
- Lacks friends
- Dislikes his job or is unemployed
- Drinks heavily or abuses other drugs
- Grew up in a violent home
- Is authoritarian toward people who are unable to defend themselves
- Is moody
- Punches walls
- Was a violent boy
- Treats others violently
- Shows contempt for women in his family or women in general

Regarding spousal abuse and churches, The *Register* article observes: "Domestic violence remains largely in the back pew . . . women . . . are moral and theological hot potatoes tossed around behind a screen of Christian culture and family values, say both Christian and secular counselors."

Need we state that God's Word in no way defends wife abuse? There is no compelling reason for a Christian woman to allow herself to be mistreated for the sake of Christianity. Scripture has to be twisted or taken wildly out of context to justify shoving a woman into the teeth of degradation and bodily harm. Clearly marriage is an institution worthy of wholehearted commitment, a heartfelt pledge to pray and love and seek wise counsel. But nowhere in God's Word do we read that "family values" are supposed to be cherished at the risk of life and limb.

Perhaps you aren't sure just what abuse is. Do you wonder if your situation fits into the category of sexual or physical abuse? Please consider the following questions.

1. Do you and your partner argue often?
2. If either of you drink, are your personalities different when you're drinking?
3. Does your partner ever lose his or her temper, throw things, or threaten you?
4. Do arguments ever end in pushing, shoving, or slapping?
5. Has your partner ever used a fist or weapon to hurt you?
6. Have you ever felt the safety of your children threatened?

If you have answered yes to two or more of these questions, you need to recognize that your home life is marred by violence. If so, and you suspect that you and/or your children are at risk, please consider taking the following steps. (Also, refer to the appendix for further assistance.)

CREATE A PLAN

Where can you go for protection when the time comes? Make a list of neighbors, friends, relatives, and local shelters, including names and phone numbers. Alert those whose names you've included. Help them understand that when and if it happens there will probably be no advance warning of your arrival.

PACK A SUITCASE

If you dare take the risk, let the batterer know you intend to leave when you think abuse is impending. Advise him (or her) that you will return home when you feel it is safe to do so. When your partner is willing to seek professional help, perhaps you won't be forced to seek refuge. (Even that is no guarantee of safety, however.)

DO NOT WARN THE ABUSER IF YOU BELIEVE HIS RESPONSE WILL BE VIOLENT

Family abuse is one of the worst crises those who experience it will have to face, and everyone involved is a victim. Children suffer its effects throughout their lives. Wives live in pain, shame, and secrecy. Husbands operate on a bitter cycle of self-hatred and deadly rage. If ever there was a time for reaching out for help from God and trustworthy friends and family, an abusive crisis is it. Please read on to learn more about trustworthy people.

STRUGGLING WITH GOD

An interesting story about crisis appears in Genesis 32:22–30. Jacob had been struggling for control all his life, initially at home with his twin brother, Esau, and later with his relative Laban. He had fought hard for the family inheritance (which he usurped from Esau) and for the woman he loved. Now, he is about to experience the most fateful confrontation of his life, again with his brother. At this point of crisis Jacob is met by God, who has taken the form of a man. Jacob doesn't recognize God at first, and he wrestles with Him all night.

Jacob must have been a pretty good wrestler. God couldn't overpower him in the human form He had taken on. But He crippled Jacob, leaving His unforgettable mark in his flesh. Finally recognizing the "man" as His Creator, Jacob demands a blessing. God complies and changes Jacob's name to Israel, a Hebrew name reflecting the statement God made concerning Jacob: "You have struggled with God and with men and have overcome."

In our times of crisis, we, like Jacob, must recognize that, ultimately, we are wrestling with God. As the Supreme Being who rules over our lives He is at work within us "to will and to act according to his good pleasure" (Philippians 2:13). He can bring good even out of tragedy.

Although we may find ourselves struggling with unpleasant circumstances, people, and emotions, it is really God who controls our lives. We must trust Him and allow Him to have His way. Ultimately, He will end the struggle. If we ask Him to, He will bless us with a new identity, a renewed hope for the future, and an entrance into His promises.

ENCOUNTERING A PERSONAL CRISIS

When we find ourselves facing overwhelming circumstances, there are steps we can take that will enable us to bring God's powerful love into the crisis.

1. Take time out to focus on God, the elements of the crisis, and your emotional reaction.
First focus on God—on who He is and His authority in your life. If you can bring yourself to thank Him—even in your

pain—for His care and provision, you will find a measure of peace. A simple prayer, "Lord, help! Guide my thoughts, direct my actions, give me strength, and take away my fear!" will open the door for His intervention.

Look at the elements of the crisis. What is actually happening? It might be helpful to put in writing all that has occurred, the threats that seem to be looming, and their potential implications.

Consider your emotional reactions. What are your feelings? How can you control your emotions in order to act more responsibly or wisely?

2. Consider all possible options.

The circumstances themselves may be unchangeable. If so, you will have to accept whatever you cannot change. Then you need to consider the things you may be able to impact with your actions or words. Is communication a factor? What can you say or do that will alleviate the situation? What resources can you draw upon?

Emotionally, you will need to fight the crippling effects of denial or depression. Somehow, with God's help, you must find the inner strength to face the facts. Controllers may be inclined toward actions that allow them to hide from their pain, whereas dependents are likely to become immersed in pain and feel unable to function. The fear of communicating, of trying and not succeeding, of reaching out and being rejected all may hinder you from doing what needs to be done. But you need to try anyway!

3. Turn to a trustworthy person or persons for support.

The Bible says "Two are better than one. . . . If one falls down his friend can help him up. But pity the man who falls and has no one to help him up!" (Ecclesiastes 4:9–10). Crisis is the time to reach out to loved ones and friends. But crisis is also the time to ask yourself some important questions: Who can I trust with this problem? Who is trustworthy? What is a trustworthy person?

RECOGNIZING TRUSTWORTHY PEOPLE

Crises come and go. Circumstances carry us into unfamiliar surroundings. New people come into our lives. People we've known for years seem to have matured. Friends or family members become new believers in Christ, or spend time in therapy or recovery groups. They say that they are making a new start. What is our response? We have to be open, but we have to be wise. What are some things to look for when we are seeking safety in relationships?

1. A trustworthy person values intimacy.

Intimacy is connectedness based on the real me, not the idealized me. Trustworthy people are not ashamed to be in touch with their need for relationships and are willing to bring the truth of who they are—both good and bad—into the picture. They are actively involved in a growth process with others and with God. Free self-disclosure and open transparency are requirements of intimacy.

Loveless power people are isolated and rarely feel loved. When they are honest about their relationships, they have to acknowledge that the people who stick with them are there out of fear, guilt, dependency, or compulsion. We can't take away people's freedom and be loved by them at the same time.

Powerless love people don't own their personal truth. For various reasons they have never developed the ability to set limits or to say no. They are defenseless in a world of control, manipulation, and exploitation. They tend to go through life compliant on the outside but resentful in their hearts. Intimacy, as we have defined it, is an impossibility for them.

Intimacy can only happen when two free individuals embrace, salute, and foster one another.

"Many a man claims to have unfailing love, but a faithful man, who can find?" (Proverbs 20:6).

2. A trustworthy person values personal accountability and responsibility.

"Safe" individuals do not have a sense of entitlement, the feeling that their needs and wants are someone else's responsibility. They know where, so to speak, to draw the line between themselves and others. Boundaries make it possible for two people to have closeness while each safely maintains his or her personal identity.

David Richo says: "In a healthy person, loyalty has its limits and unconditional love can exist with conditional involvement. Unconditional does not, after all, mean uncritical. You can both love someone unconditionally and place conditions upon your interactions to protect your own boundaries. 'I love you unconditionally and I take care of myself by not living with you.'"[3]

A boundary is an invisible protective fence keeping out abuse and control and preventing others from doing things to us that we don't want them to do. A boundary's purpose is not to keep people away, but to foster relationships in which I am not controlled or controlling. In healthy relationships, the innate identity that is me is not bestowed by others (powerless love) or plundered by them (loveless power.) Self-control, rather than "other" control, becomes my goal.

"For each one should carry his own load" (Galatians 6:5).

"A prudent man sees danger and takes refuge, but the simple keep going and suffer for it" (Proverbs 22:3).

3. A trustworthy person is teachable.

Beware of the person who has no problems, who has nothing to learn. These know-it-alls invariably become the biggest problems of all. Also, watch out for men and women who say "my life is your problem." Their philosophy is that it is your job to take care of them. That way they don't have to try. It's not necessary for them to learn anything.

The powerful lover exhibits the attitude of humility, and humility is a prerequisite to learning. Humility acknowledges that there is much to be discovered about self as well as others. Trustworthy people realize that they are in a growth process, that their perspective is incomplete, that they hold only partial truth when they face any issue. These people hunger and thirst after righteousness in their relationships with God, self, and others.

"Pride only breeds quarrels, but wisdom is found in those who take advice" (Proverbs 13:10).

"A wise son heeds his father's instruction, but a mocker does not listen to rebuke" (Proverbs 13:1).

"Whoever gives heed to instruction prospers, and blessed is he who trusts in the Lord" (Proverbs 16:20).

"He who speaks before listening—that is his folly and his shame" (Proverbs 18:13).

"Listen to advice and accept instruction, and in the end you will be wise" (Proverbs 19:20).

4. A trustworthy person values honesty.

The powerful lover's own thoughts, feelings, and stages of growth are important to him. His self-image accurately reflects his real self, so self-deception is minimal. "Safe" people have identified their defenses and are in the process of laying them down.

Honesty is an important component of a trustworthy person's relationship with you. They are not interested in grace without truth. They acknowledge that confronting is crucial to a healthy, maturing relationship.

"Wounds from a friend can be trusted, but an enemy multiplies kisses" (Proverbs 27:6).

"He who conceals his sins does not prosper, but whoever confesses and renounces them finds mercy" (Proverbs 28:13).

"A rebuke impresses a man of discernment more than a hundred lashes a fool" (Proverbs 17:10).

5. A trustworthy person does not reject us because of our unfinished parts.

As we've noted before, each of us is like a gigantic iceberg. The tip of the iceberg looks pristine and clean. When we idealize ourselves and others, we are only focusing on the tip of the iceberg. When we are honest, we know that there are also guilt, anger, shame, and depression in us, and perhaps even an addictive and/or compulsive aspect to our character. Remember God's truth: "There is no one righteous, not even one" (Romans 3:10).

Can individuals connect with your unfinished parts, or do they say, "I only want the other part of you—the part that looks so good." If that is their perspective, their love is conditional and they are full of judgment. There is no security in a relationship with them. Loneliness that has been hidden, fears that have been buried, and wishes that have been overlooked cannot be brought to these people. If you make yourself vulnerable, you will be crushed.

By contrast, trustworthy men and women are willing to offer acceptance and forgiveness to you, because they know all too well how much they have been forgiven.

"What you have seen with your eyes do not bring hastily to court, for what will you do in the end if your neighbor puts you to shame?" (Proverbs 25:7b–8).

"Who can say, 'I have kept my heart pure; I am clean and without sin'?" (Proverbs 20:9).

"A friend loveth at all times, and a brother is born for adversity" (Proverbs 17:17).

7. A trustworthy person experiences life vividly "with full concentration and total absorption" (Abraham Maslow).

Some people are "present" in every situation. They live in the here and now. Their lives are neither totally focused on the past nor on the future. Rather than awaiting what will be, or bemoaning what could have been, they embrace what is.

"This is the day that the Lord has made; let us rejoice and be glad in it" (Psalm 118:24).

"Do not boast about tomorrow, for you do not know what a day may bring forth" (Proverbs 27:1).

8. A trustworthy person has proven himself to be reliable.

This person's life consists of more than good intentions. His words and actions are congruent—he walks his talk and talks his walk. The lives of trustworthy people can be observed and tested without the threat of defenses or denial. This doesn't for one minute mean that these individuals don't make mistakes and fail. They have learned from past mistakes, and because they are growing, they don't deny their failures, minimize them, excuse them, or continue them.

Each of us would be wise to treat a new relationship as if it were the flashing yellow light at an intersection. We don't want to stop permanently and never risk making a move. And we don't want to barrel through and desperately hope it's safe. A yellow light means we pause and proceed with caution. It means we give a person a little of our heart and observe what he (or she) does with it. In 1 John 4:1 we are commanded to "test the spirits." It would serve many of us well to follow that admonition in our relationships.

"A righteous man is cautious in friendship, but the way of the wicked leads them astray" (Proverbs 12:26).

"It is not good to have zeal without knowledge, nor to be hasty and miss the way. A man's own folly ruins his life, yet his heart rages against the Lord" (Proverbs 19:2–3).

9. A trustworthy person has great respect for individual autonomy and separateness.

Trustworthy people understand that we must be separate in order to be close. In a maturing relationship, both people are becoming more separate; they are forming their identity as distinct from the other person's. Carl Whitaker puts it this way: "As two people live together . . . they grow closer together and farther apart at the same rate. This is a weird kind of business, but the closer they get, the more separate they are. If they don't grow more separate, they can't grow closer. If they can't increase their individuality, they can't increase their oneness . . . the more you are free to be with . . . significant others, the more you are free to be with yourself. The more you are with you the more you can be with her."[4]

It bears repeating: one must be independent before one can move toward interdependence. Safety is directly related to our "emerging from being enmeshed into others, from losing our selfhood in others, from getting hooked by others, from feeling fused to others and becoming free to be with others as distinct and differing persons."[5]

Trustworthy people value both closeness and space. They can relate intimately with others while maintaining their sense of self. Even God establishes His separateness from us. His thoughts are different from our thoughts, His ways are different from our ways. Yet He longs for relationship with us.

"Seldom set foot in your neighbor's house—too much of you, and he will hate you" (Proverbs 25:17).

10. A trustworthy person brings out the best in me.

Something happens inside me when I am in the presence of someone who doesn't place his conditions on me and doesn't condemn, control, or discount me. My involvement with this person enables me to be more honest, more responsible, more thoughtful, and more caring. If I leave the company of another human being cut to pieces, crazier, or compulsive, he (or she) is not a safe person for me.

"The purposes of a man's heart are deep waters, but a man of understanding draws them out" (Proverbs 20:5).

Obviously not one of us has "arrived." But we are moving in the direction of becoming trustworthy people ourselves, while at the same time becoming aware of the personal and emotional integrity of others. We're sure you've seen by now that the powerful love of Jesus Christ, which we've been talking about all along, is the key to becoming a trustworthy man or woman. He is the only totally trustworthy person who has ever lived.

As we try to live out our daily lives in reliance on our own strength and wisdom, we will inevitably be either controlled or controlling. Powerful love is the natural consequence of communion with God and with His people. As we let God have more of us, He is ready to give us more of Himself. With the Holy Spirit's guidance and empowering, we can become the powerful lovers God has called us to be—Christ's feet, arms, hands, legs, smile, ears and eyes— bringing His love to a hurting world.

It is our prayer that you will join us on our journey toward powerful love.

NOTES

1. Elisabeth Kubler-Ross, *Questions and Answers on Death and Dying* (New York: Macmillan, 1974).
2. Melissa Balmain Weiner, "The Abusive Male," *Orange County Register* (20 October 1991), Close-Up section, 1.
3. David Richo, "Maintaining Personal Boundaries in Relationship," *The California Therapist*, July-August 1990, 40.
4. Carl Whitaker in John R. Neill and David P. Kniskern, eds., *From Psyche to System: The Evolving Therapy of Carl Whitaker* (New York: Guilford, 1982), 172.
5. David Augsburger, *Sustaining Love* (Ventura, Calif.: Regal, 1988), 170.

RESOURCES AND REFERENCES

SCRIPTURES ABOUT COMMUNICATION

"Then Job replied, 'How long will you torment me and crush me with words?'" (Job 19:2).

"Reckless words pierce like a sword, but the tongue of the wise brings healing" (Proverbs 12:18).

"The tongue that brings healing is a tree of life, but a deceitful tongue crushes the spirit" (Proverbs 15:4).

"The tongue has the power of life and death, and those who love it will eat its fruits" (Proverbs 18:21).

"He who guards his mouth and his tongue keeps himself from calamity" (Proverbs 21:23).

"If you argue your case with a neighbor, do not betray another man's confidence, or he who hears it may shame you and you will never lose your bad reputation" (Proverbs 25:9–10).

"A word aptly spoken is like apples of gold in settings of silver" (Proverbs 25:11).

"Through patience a ruler can be persuaded, and a gentle tongue can break a bone" (Proverbs 25:15).

"A lying tongue hates those it hurts, and a flattering mouth works ruin" (Proverbs 26:28).

"Let another praise you, and not your own mouth; someone else and not your own lips" (Proverbs 27:2).

"He who rebukes a man will in the end gain more favor than he who has a flattering tongue" (Proverbs 28:23).

"A fool gives full vent to his anger, but a wise man keeps himself under control" (Proverbs 29:11).

"She [a wife of noble character] speaks with wisdom, and faithful instruction is on her tongue" (Proverbs 31:26).

"My dear brothers, take note of this: Everyone should be quick to listen, slow to speak and slow to become angry, for man's anger does not bring about the righteous life that God desires" (James 1:19–20).

"If anyone considers himself religious and yet does not keep a tight rein on his tongue, he deceives himself and his religion is worthless" (James 1:26).

"The tongue is a small part of the body but it makes great boasts. Consider what a great forest is set on fire by a small spark. The tongue also is a fire, a world of evil among the parts of the body. It corrupts the whole person, sets the whole course of his life on fire, and is itself set on fire by hell.
"All kinds of animals, birds, reptiles and creatures of the sea are being tamed and have been tamed by man, but no man can tame the tongue. It is a restless evil, full of deadly poison.
"With the tongue we praise our Lord and Father, and with it we curse men, who have been made in God's likeness. Out of

the same mouth come praise and cursing. My brothers, this should not be" (James 3:5–10).

"What causes fights and quarrels among you? Don't they come from your desires that battle within you? You want something but don't get it. You kill and covet but you cannot have what you want. You quarrel and fight. You do not have, because you do not ask God" (James 4:1–2).

"But the wisdom that comes from heaven is first of all pure; then peace-loving, considerate, submissive, full of mercy and good fruit, impartial and sincere" (James 3:17).

"Finally, all of you, live in harmony with one another; be sympathetic, love as brothers, be compassionate and humble. Do not repay evil with evil, or insult with insult, but with blessing, because to this you were called so that you may inherit a blessing. For, 'whoever would love life and see good days must keep his tongue from evil and his lips from deceitful speech'" (1 Peter 3:8–10).

"The entire law is summed up in a single command: 'Love your neighbor as yourself.' If you keep on biting and devouring each other, watch out or you will be destroyed by each other" (Galatians 5:14–15).

"Therefore each of you must put off falsehood and speak truthfully to his neighbor, for we are all members of one body" (Ephesians 4:25).

"'In your anger do not sin': Do not let the sun go down while you are still angry, and do not give the devil a foothold" (Ephesians 4:26–27).

"Do not let any unwholesome talk come out of your mouths, but only what is helpful for building others up according to their needs, that it may benefit those who listen. And do not grieve the Holy Spirit of God, with whom you were sealed for the day of redemption. Get rid of all bitterness, rage and anger, brawling and slander, along with every form of malice. Be kind and compassionate to one another, forgiving each other, just as in Christ God forgave you" (Ephesians 4:29–32).

THE FRUIT OF THE SPIRIT IN RELATIONSHIPS

LOVE: Can I see beyond myself, my needs, and my feelings in this relationship?

JOY: Are there times of laughter, lightness, and fun?

PEACE: Is there a quietness and honesty in my soul? Is there the security that even in the midst of conflict we are supportive of one another?

LONGSUFFERING: Am I open to others' point of view? Can I accept differences without feeling threatened?

KINDNESS: Do I direct kind words and actions toward others? Do I speak kindly of others when they aren't around?

GOODNESS: Am I attempting to be God's love-connection?

FAITHFULNESS: Am I committed to unconditional love and loyalty?

GENTLENESS: Do I treat others with the tenderness I'd like to feel from them? Am I careful with their sensitivities?

SELF-CONTROL: Do I avoid using my emotions to manipulate or attack? Am I taking my responsibility in every relationship?

GOD'S WORD ABOUT "PUTTING ON" AND "PUTTING OFF"

PUT OFF		PUT ON	
Lack of love	1 John 4:7–8, 20	John 15:12	Love
Doubt	1 Thess. 5:24	Heb. 11:1	Faith
Worry	Matt. 6:25–32	1 Pet. 5:7	Trust
Lack of rejoicing	Phil. 4:4	1 Thess. 5:16	Rejoicing
Hypocrisy	Job 8:13 KJV	Eph. 4:25	Honesty
Complacency	James 4:17	Col. 3:23	Diligence
Evil thoughts	Prov. 23:6–7	Phil. 4:8	Positive thoughts
Profanity	Ps. 109:17	1 Tim. 4:12	Edification
Lying	Eph. 4:25	Zech. 8:16	Speaking truth
Gossip	1 Tim. 5:13	Rom. 14:19	Positive speech
Hatred	Matt. 5:21–22	1 Cor. 13:3	Kindness, love
Wrath	James 1:19–20	Gal. 5:22–23	Self-control
Losing temper	Prov. 16:32	Rom. 5:3–4	Self-control
Jealousy	Prov. 27:4	1 Cor. 13:4–5	Preferring others
Complaining	Jude 15–16	Heb. 13:5, 15	Contentment
Murmuring	Prov. 19:3	1 Cor. 10:10	Gratefulness
Discontent	Phil. 4:11–13	Heb. 13:5	Satisfaction
Impatience	James 1:2–4	Luke 21:19	Patience
Ungratefulness	Rom. 1:21	Eph. 5:20	Thankfulness
Conceit	1 Tim. 3:6	James 4:6	Humility
Pride	1 Cor. 4:7	Prov. 27:2	Humility
Unforgiveness	Mark 11:25	Matt. 6:14	Forgiveness
Judging	Matt. 7:1–2	John 8:7–9; 15:22	Self-examination
Bitterness	Heb. 12:15	Col. 3:12	Tenderheartedness

"Who we are profoundly affects the significance of our communication and the quality of our relationships."

FOR ABUSE VICTIMS

WHEN NOT TO RECONCILE

Don't reconcile with your partner if

- He/she refuses to go to counseling.
- He/she drops out of counseling or has to be coerced to continue.
- He/she continues to be violent.
- He/she continues to threaten you.
- He/she feels no remorse for the damage done to you.
- He/she blames you for his/her lack of control.
- He/she continues to abuse substances.
- He/she uses your vulnerability in counseling sessions against you.
- He/she accuses you of having affairs.
- He/she follows you, refuses to listen to your limits, and/or monitors what you do.
- He/she tries to make you grateful, saying things like, "I haven't hit you in two months. What more do you want?"
- He/she refuses to listen to your expression of anger about the abuse. Perhaps you are accused of "rubbing it in." Or you are threatened that your talking about the abuse will make it happen again.
- He/she agrees to go to counseling only if you are there to motivate him/her.
- He/she continues to isolate you and gets in the way of your efforts to connect with others.
- He/she acts out in front of the children.
- He/she blames you for his/her choices.
- He/she tells the kids that you hold grudges.
- He/she turns the kids into detectives.
- He/she threatens to fight you for child custody.
- He/she blames you for separating from him and lets the children know that it's "Mommy's fault" or "Daddy's fault" that he/she is unable to see them.

- He/she shows up for visitation unexpectedly and becomes disturbed when you don't fit into his schedule.
- He/she is persistently late for visitation.
- He/she "forgets" to show up for visitation or cancels previously made plans at the last minute.
- He/she tries to buy the kids' affection.
- He/she accuses you of leaving him for someone else in front of the kids.
- He/she starts to take out his aggressiveness on the children.

SIGNS OF POSSIBLE POSITIVE CHANGE

The word "possible" must be stressed, because it is always useful to act a certain way to get what one wants without undergoing fundamental, long-term changes in attitudes and beliefs. However, take a second look if

- He/she has stopped using physical force, threats, or others forms of intimidation for at least six months.
- You can disagree with him/her without incurring wrath.
- You can say no to sex without apology.
- He/she sees the necessity for you to have a support system and outside interests.
- He/she no longer blames you for what isn't working in his/her life.
- He/she no longer shames or humiliates you.
- He/she listens and values you opinion.
- He/she has stopped denying, hiding, or minimizing his/her abuse.
- He/she has maintained positive changes over a period of at least six months.
- He/she has faced his/her issues with a wise counselor.

HELPFUL BOOKS

Arterburn, Stephen, and David Stoop. *When Someone You Love Is Someone You Hate.* Waco, Tex.: Word, 1988.

Augsburger, David. *Cherishable Love and Marriage.* Scottsdale, Pa.: Herald, 1958.

_____. *Sustaining Love.* Ventura, Calif.: Regal, 1988.

Bader, Ellyn, and Peter Pearson. *In Quest of the Mystical Mate.* New York: Brunner/Mazel, 1988.

Beattie, Melody. *Beyond Codependency.* New York: Harper & Row, 1989.

_____. *Codependent No More.* New York: Harper & Row, 1987.

Beck, Aaron T. *Love Is Never Enough.* New York: Harper & Row, 1988.

Campbell, Susan M. *Beyond the Power Struggle.* San Luis Obispo, Calif.: Impact, 1984.

Carter, Les. *Imperative People.* Nashville: Thomas Nelson, 1991.

_____. *The Push-Pull Marriage.* Grand Rapids: Baker, 1983.

Clinebell, Howard J., and Charlotte H. Clinebell. *The Intimate Marriage.* New York: Harper & Row, 1970.

Congo, David; Janet Congo; Paul Meier; and Frank Minirth. *A Walk with the Serenity Prayer.* Nashville: Thomas Nelson, 1991.

Congo, David, and Janet Congo. *Free to Soar.* Old Tappan, N.J.: Revell, 1987.

_____. *Less Stress.* Ventura, Calif.: Regal, 1986.

Congo, Jan. *Free to Be God's Woman.* Ventura, Calif.: Regal, 1985.

Congo, Janet; Julie Mask; and Jan Meier. *The Woman Within.* Nashville: Nelson Comm. 1992.

Covey, Stephen. *Principle-Centered Leadership.* New York: Summit, 1991.

_____. *The Seven Habits of Highly Effective People.* New York: Simon & Schuster, 1989.

Evans, Patricia. *The Verbally Abusive Relationship.* Holbrook, Mass.: Bob Adams, 1992.

Forward, Susan, and Joan Torres. *Men Who Hate Women and the Women Who Love Them.* New York: Bantam, 1987.

Foster, Richard. *Money, Sex and Power.* New York: Harper & Row, 1985.

Groom, Nancy. *From Bondage to Bonding.* Colorado Springs: NavPress, 1991.

_____. *Married Without Masks.* Colorado Springs: NavPress, 1989.

Hendricks, Gay, and Kathleen Hendricks. *Conscious Loving: The Journey to Commitment.* New York: Bantam, 1990.

Hendrix, Harville. *Getting the Love You Want.* New York: Harper & Row, 1988.

Jones, Ann, and Susan Schechter. *When Love Goes Wrong.* New York: HarperCollins, 1992.

Jones, Riki. *The Empowered Woman.* New York: Shapolosky, 1992.

Kiley, Dan. *What to Do When He Won't Change.* New York: Putnam, 1987.

Lerner, Harriet Goldhor. *The Dance of Anger.* New York: Harper & Row, 1985.

_____. *The Dance of Intimacy.* New York: Harper & Row, 1989.

Lewis, C. S. *The Four Loves.* San Diego, Calif.: Harcourt Brace Jovanovich, 1988.

Mallinger, Allan, and Jeannette DeWyze. *Too Perfect.* New York: Clarkson Potter, 1992.

McKay, Matthew; Peter Rogers; and Judith McKay. *When Anger Hurts.* Oakland, Calif.: New Harbinger, 1989.

Milwid, Beth. *Working with Men.* New York: Berkley, 1990.

Oliver, Gary Jackson, and H. Norman Wright. *When Anger Hits Home.* Chicago: Moody, 1992.

Penner, Clifford, and Joyce Penner. *The Gift of Sex.* Waco, Tex.: Word, 1981.

Peters, Thomas, and Robert Waterman. *In Search of Excellence.* New York: Warner, 1982.

Schneider, Jennifer. *Back from Betrayal.* New York: Ballantine, 1988.

Strom, Kay Marshall. *In the Name of Submission.* Portland, Oreg.: Multnomah, 1986.

Swindoll, Charles. *The Quest for Character.* Portland, Oreg.: Multnomah, 1990.

Viscott, David. *Emotionally Free.* Chicago: Contemporary, 1992.

Waitley, Dennis. *The Double Win.* Old Tappan, N.J.: Revell, 1985.

Weiner-Davis, Michele. *Divorce-Busting.* New York: Summit, 1992.

Wiwcharuck, Peter. *Building Effective Leadership.* Three Hills, Alberta: International Christian Leadership Development Corporation, 1987.

OTHER RESOURCES

TWELVE-STEP GROUPS

Adult Children of Alcoholics
Central Service Board
Box 35623
Los Angeles, CA 90035

Al-Anon/Alateen
Family Group Headquarters, Inc.
Box 182
Madison Square Station
New York, NY 10159
(800) 356-9996

See also listing below under "Alcohol and Drug Abuse."

Alcoholics Anonymous
Box 459
Grand Central Station
New York, NY 10163
(212) 686-1100
Hours: 9:00–5:00 EST

Emotions Anonymous
Box 4245
St. Paul, MN 55104
(612) 647-9712

Co-Dependents Anonymous
Box 33577
Phoenix, AZ 85067
(602) 277-7991

Families Anonymous
Box 528
Van Nuys, CA 91408
(818) 989-7841

Incest Survivors Anonymous
Box 5613
Long Beach, CA 90017

See also listings below under "Abuse and Violence."

Overcomers Outreach
2290 W. Whittier Blvd.
Suite D
La Habra, CA 90631
(213) 697-3994

Sexaholics Anonymous
Box 300
Simi Valley, CA 93062

Minirth-Meier Clinics
(800) 545-1819

There are Minirth-Meier Clinics throughout the United States offering treatment in a hospital setting, partial hospital programs, and counseling centers that match the individual needs of the person with the strengths and specialities of the counselor. For information, call the above number.

ABUSE AND VIOLENCE

The National Domestic Violence Toll-Free Hotline
c/o Michigan Coalition Against Domestic Violence
P.O. Box 7032
Huntington Woods, MI 48070
1-800-333-7233
1-800-873-6363 TDD Number for the hearing impaired

Call toll-free, twenty-four hours a day for information or referral to a support group or battered women's shelter anywhere in the United States.

The National Coalition Against Domestic Violence
P.O. Box 15127
Washington, D.C. 20003-0127
(202) 638-6388

A coalition, made up of individuals and organizations, that works for battered women and provides information about domestic violence.

National Clearinghouse for the Defense of Battered Women
125 South 9th St., Suite 302
Philadelphia, PA 19107
(215) 351-0010

Provides legal information to women charged with crimes for defending themselves from abuse and to their attorneys.

State Toll-Free Domestic Violence Hotlines

(These numbers are toll-free if you live in one of these states.)

Arkansas	1-800-332-4443
Indiana	1-800-334-7233
Nevada	1-800-992-5757
New Hampshire	1-800-852-3311
New Jersey	1-800-572-7233
New York	1-800-942-6906 (English)
	1-800-942-6908 (Spanish)
North Dakota	1-800-472-2911
Oklahoma	1-800-522-7233
Washington	1-800-562-6025
Wisconsin	1-800-333-7233

Ending Men's Violence Task Group
C/O RAVEN
P.O. Box 24159
St. Louis, MO 63130
(314) 725-6137

Provides counseling for abusive men and publishes and distributes *Ending Men's Violence National Referral Directory,* which lists programs for men nationwide.

Center for the Prevention of Sexual and Domestic Violence
1914 North 39th St., Suite 205
Seattle, WA 98103

Provides resources addressing religious issues that arise for victims of sexual and domestic violence and for abusers.

National Committee for Prevention of Child Abuse
P.O. Box 94283
Chicago, IL 60690
(312) 663-3520

Offers a free catalog of about sixty publications on topics including parenting, child abuse, and child abuse prevention. Provides referrals to chapters in every state.

Child Help National Child Abuse Hotline
1-800-422-4453

Provides information about child abuse and neglect and reporting laws. Offers referrals to treatment facilities for children, parents, and adult survivors of abuse.

Incest Survivors Anonymous
P.O. Box 5613
Long Beach, CA 90805-0613
(213) 428-5599
Hours: Wednesday and Friday afternoons PST

Makes referrals to local groups and offers information and support.

VOICES (Victims of Incest Can Emerge As Survivors)
Box 148309
Chicago, IL 60614
(312) 327-1500

Provides information about VOICES chapters around the country. For information, write or leave a message with your address.

Parents Anonymous
6733 South Sepulveda Blvd., Suite 270
Los Angeles, CA 90045
1-800-421-0353

Provides information about child abuse and referrals to local sup-port groups for parents who abuse or fear they may abuse their children.

PARENTAL KIDNAPPING

National Center for Missing and Exploited Children
2101 Wilson Blvd., Suite 550
Arlington, VA 22201
1-800-843-5678

Hotline provides information, including publications and re-sources, and technical assistance to parents who are searching for missing children or trying to prevent parental abduction.

Child Find, Inc.
P.O. Box 277
New Paltz, NY 12561
1-800-I AM LOST

Provides referrals to help locate lost children or find support and legal advice.

CHILD SUPPORT

Handbook for Child Support Enforcement
Dept. 628M
Consumer Information Center
Pueblo, CO 81009

Write for a copy of the handbook.

The Child Support Enforcement Network
(301) 833-0054
Hours: 9:00–5:00 EST

Provides information about state and federal laws.

Child Support
119 Nicodemus Rd.
Reistertown, MD 21136

Provides information by mail about state and federal laws and referral to local agencies for help with enforcement.

DIVORCE

Parents Without Partners
8807 Colesville Rd.
Silver Spring, MD 20910
1-800-637-7974

Provides information and referral to local groups that are open to anyone who has been separated thirty days or more.

CAREER EDUCATION

Displaced Homemakers Network
1411 K St., N.W., Suite 930
Washington, D.C. 20005
(202) 628-6767

Makes referrals to local groups that help women with career education and job training.

AIDS

AIDS Hotline
1-800-342-2437
1-800-876-2437
1-800-922-2437

Provides information about HIV and AIDS and referrals to local advocacy groups, physicians, treatment facilities, and test sites.

AIDS Project Inform
347 Dolores St., Suite 301
San Francisco, CA 94110
1-800-822-7422
In San Francisco: (415) 558-9051
Hours: 10:00–2:00 PST

Provides information about drug treatment for those who are HIV positive or who have AIDS.

National Sexually Transmitted Diseases Hotline
1-800-227-8922
Hours: 8:00–11:00 EST

Offers referrals to local groups and information about sexually transmitted diseases, testing sites, and treatment facilities.

AIDS Resource Ministry
12488 Venice Blvd.
Los Angeles, CA 90631

Exodus Ministry
P.O. Box 2121
San Rafael, CA 94912

Spatula Ministries
P.O. Box 444
La Habra, CA 90631

An organization for parents and loved ones of homosexuals/ lesbians.

ALCOHOL AND DRUG ABUSE

Alcoholics Anonymous World Services
P.O. Box 459
Grand Central Station
New York, NY 10163
(212) 686-1100
Hours: 9:00–5:00 EST

Provides the numbers of state groups that can refer you to a local program.

Al-Anon Family Group World Services
P.O. Box 862
Midtown Station
New York, NY 10018-0862
(212) 302-7240
Hours: 9:00–4:00 EST, Monday through Friday

Provides information for family and friends of alcoholics and referrals to state and local programs.

Alateen
Same address and phone as Al-Anon

Provides information and referrals to local groups for teenagers.

Alcohol and Drug Counseling
1-800-ALCOHOL

Makes referrals to local alcohol or drug counselors and recovery groups.

National Council on Alcoholism
12 West 21st St.
New York, NY 10010
(212) 206-6770

Write or phone for a comprehensive list of publications and resources (including publications on women and alcoholism and fetal alcohol syndrome). Provides referral to the nearest local council that offers treatment and support programs or information on local resources.

National Institute on Drug Abuse
Information and Treatment Referral Hotline
1-800-662-HELP
Hours: 9:00–3:00 EST, Monday through Friday
           12:00 NOON–3:00 A.M. EST, Saturday and Sunday

Provides referrals to local alcohol and drug counselors, support groups, and treatment facilities.

National Cocaine Hotline
1-800-COCAINE

Provides information about cocaine and makes referrals to local treatment programs.

Cocaine Anonymous
1-800-347-8998

Offers referrals to local groups or treatment facilities.

For more information regarding materials, seminars,
or speaking engagements, write or call:

Free To Soar Seminars
P.O. Box 4271
Mission Veijo, CA 92691-2271
1-714-830-CARE